SWING TRADING

Guide To Investing In Financial Markets, To Create Passive Income, Secrets, And Strategies To Profit

Scott McMoney

This document is geared towards providing exact and reliable information with regards to the topic and issue covered. The publication is sold with the idea that the publisher is not required to render accounting, officially permitted, or otherwise, qualified services. If advice is necessary, legal or professional, a practiced individual in the profession should be ordered.

- From a Declaration of Principles which was accepted and approved equally by a Committee of the American Bar Association and a Committee of Publishers and Associations.

The information provided herein is stated to be truthful and consistent, in that any liability, in terms of inattention or otherwise, by any usage or abuse of any policies, processes, or directions contained within is the solitary and utter responsibility of the recipient reader. Under no circumstances will any legal responsibility or blame be held against the publisher for any reparation, damages, or monetary loss due to the information herein, either directly or indirectly.

TABLE OF CONTENTS

INTRODUCTION 1

CHAPTER 1 : WHAT IS SWING TRADING? 5

CHAPTER 2 : HISTORICAL EVENTS IN THE FX MARKET ... 28

CHAPTER 3 : BASIC TECHNICAL RULES................................. 46

CHAPTER 4 : FUNDAMENTAL TRADING STRATIGIES 61

CHAPTER 5 : SELECTING STOCKS FOR SWING TRADING .. 94

CHAPTER 6 : DAY TRADING AND SWING TRADING - THE DIFFERENCE 127

CONCLUSION 133

INTRODUCTION

Swinging reminds me of watching the waves on the shore of the ocean. Each wave has a crest and a trough a motion that imitates up and down the movement of stocks from high to low or small. Swing traders do not attempt to surf this wave by moving close to the top but by sailing from a trough to a top as in the Perfect Storm scenes.

Swing is not a new concept. It has become a viable strategy for the average investor only recently. Only a few with access to an exchange floor could make short-term trades in and out from positions every day until the Internet opened up the markets for virtually everyone.

In that pre-Internet age, there simply were no real-time quotes or online diagram services. You must phone a stockbroker to get a bid, leave a message, and hope that your call will be returned before the market closes. The price of stocks cannot be tracked all day long because you again needed the stock dealer who had exclusive access to price details. Shift trading — moving in and out from positions to benefit from short-term market movements — was therefore not necessary.

In the 1980s, stockbrokers started to rely on an early version of automated exchange access. An old program, Quotron, supported mobile brokers with quotes far quicker than ever. It's been groundbreaking. These brokers with Quotron machines had a distinct advantage over brokers who were dependent on delayed quotes and phone quotes or on exchange floors-based ticker quotes.

By contrast with the world today, even the idea of supplying stockbrokers with their own direct access is pale. In fact, stockbrokers are redundant. Any trader who knows enough about investment and knows how to conduct a company will probably use an online discount courier service, which is so extremely simple that conventional courier services are of questionable value. The mainstream companies have stressed the need for their "analysts 'professional advice," but the record is weak. Not only did the predictions of analysts underperform the market; in certain situations, investors should have done the exact opposite of their suggestions.

Today, the old-fashioned stockbroker is slowly gone and is replaced by the mix of analysts and subscription services. The assertion that these services have some useful information is doubtful. In reality, investors now have superior free information and don't have to pay for support from online brokerage services. For example, Charles Schwab, the popular discount brokerage company, provides its traders with free access to Standard & Poors inventories, Reuters Analyst ratings, and Schwab's own stock-rating service.

Educated investors, who are most vulnerable to short-term tactics like swing trading, are the least likely to rely on other investors advice. Historically, stock-brokers, financial advisors, and analysts have been advised extremely poorly, so it is more likely today that individual investors choose to continue without assistance or advice from a contracted or subscription-based person or company.

This book addresses investors who are eager to learn the necessary steps to invest on their own. They want to master tested approaches and understand the drawbacks of relying on others to provide investment advice.

Nobody will teach you how to grow rich quickly and safely. These claims are baseless and empty. Your success rate can be improved by using tactics that will give you the edge and help to predict the next price path. There is no "safe-fire" system for 100% benefit. Swing trade will, however, boost your success rate, timing, and overall profitability.

This book also answers the question of the goods to be used for swing exchange. Most people simply believe that you must use stocks as part of a swinging trading strategy to hold long or short positions in stocks. This subject is extensively guarded. Nonetheless, buying and selling stock shares is, in practice, a restricted strategy since you are restricted to investing in a small capital pool. Later in this book, you will discover ways to increase your swing trading ability with less capital and less risk. You can also see how to take positions if you expect the stock to decrease but without selling the stock shortly. This risky approach is not the only way to play a bear market or even the safest or most economical way.

Throughout your knowledge about swing trading, you can also extend your understanding of market risk, gain insight into alternative ways to invest, and develop your business knowledge base. Swing trading is a technological technique in the short term. This does not mean it must be high-risk or suitable only for the richest or most experienced investors. Apparently, this is a technique that can be useful if people understand and value the fundamental realities of risk, timing, and investment methods.

CHAPTER 1 :
WHAT IS SWING TRADING?

How Swing Trading Works?

Everyone knows that big institutional investors, such as mutual funds, have a huge advantage over the individual investment provider more capital, better analysis, large diversification. However, you have an advantage over the major institutions in certain respects. We can not decide on the market quickly; pay attention to the small, short-term price changes which characterize market cycles; or look only at a few main stocks. Because of their scale, the large institutions will take a shotgun approach to investment.

Probably, you do not have millions of dollars in your portfolio, and nobody else needs to comment. Your advantage is this versatility and agility, and you can benefit from swing trading strategies. You work within a very short time, in most cases for two to five days, with swing trading.

You may find that the movement of stock prices appears to respond (or in particular, overreact) to any market occurrence in the short term. The range of events includes trading rates, wider market developments, and financial, economic, and political news. This rise in stock prices will be clarified later in this chapter in light of the three key emotions actually regulating the market: greed, fear, and uncertainty.

In terms of these three emotions, short-term price volatility can be identified and expected, and this is where you gain your trade advantage. Instead of choosing on the basis of greed, fear, and confusion, swinging is a rational and analytical rather than emotional strategy. An ancient adage about the market says that "Bull and bears can benefit, but pigs and chickens can't." You can make profits in any form of market, but only if you can see the emotional reactions which rule the majority's thought.

Such emotions are, in fact, primarily deciding and triggering shifts in the market's short-term prices. The unpredictable short-term pricing refutes the effective market hypothesis and assumes that all inventory pricing represents everything that we know publicly at any given time. The reality indicates that this is incorrect.

There could be an open market at a different level. For example, the long-term averages of price change may be in some degree of performance, but the two to five-day price volatility were almost entirely triggered by these three destructive emotions and their domination of market thought.

It is however rational to assume that the effective market hypothesis will, but not in the short term, be a viable theory for the long term. On the other hand, the spontaneous walking hypothesis is another business idea. This is a more fatalist business view. The random walk is the assumption that there is a 50/50 probability of a stock price rising or dropping at any given moment. The entire inventory price is assumed to be completely unpredictable.

The random walk accurately defines the tendency of stocks over two to five days. Short-term pricing explicitly responds to emotional overreaction and illogicality. Nonetheless, a study of stock prices in the long term shows a clear link between strong basic principles and high price growth (or poor fundamentals leading to price deterioration). The two key hypotheses may therefore be very instructive in interpreting stock markets in the short and long term:

1. The successful theory of the economy only makes sense in the long term. There is no clear advantage in short-term inventory pricing, shifts in inventory prices due to emotional consequences.
2. The random walking theory in the two to the five-day window makes perfect sense and explains the way stocks behave; however, it is not so much a random case but the product of a struggle between gullibility and fear of investors (with an uncertainty that represents a stalemate). In the long run, however, the random walking hypothesis falls apart.

The basic Concepts of Swing Trading

Any strategy you follow on the market will, of course, decide your progress. But investors continue to assume that certain programs maintain consistent income efficiently, and this is simply not true. Timing is the benefits center. Although it is important to accumulate fundamental stocks, it obviously takes more time than anything else to decide whether your decisions generate gains or losses.

Many people who purchase stock shares mistakenly believe that their price is a point of departure or the "zero base" of their investment. The stock is expected to through from that zero base price. But, as someone who has already invested money into stocks knows, often the stock price drop.

The program you use to pick stocks can be your real starting point; your plan governs the timing of the implementation. That's the biggest difference. If you believe in theoretical analysis or scientific analysis doesn't matter. The theory continues to be the same: the approach is used to identify the stocks you want to trade, and the technique tests your decision. Swing trading gives you an effective technique.

Shift traders take advantage of stock price trends using the timing of short-term trading patterns. These patterns include trading in short waves (so the value of the two to five-day period), during which stock prices are increasing and decreasing. After clear trends and signals, a reverse sometimes happens, and swing trading is a strong timing technique.

Such trends are known by the swing trader. The swing trader identifies a selling signal after the stock has risen in a certain trend (in the market change, the market gap in the exchange range of one day, and the volume). When the price falls in a specific pattern, the swing trader joins and purchases. This timing is counter to the current market trend and tends to expect a reversal. The natural price tendency is to work in these short periods. Since swing trading involves timing a transaction in advance that prices would do the opposite, swing trading would be a short-term form of opposite investment.

Traders are usually reactive rather than contrary. And when people see a stock going up, they want to buy, and they want to sell when they see it falling down. In contrast, Swing traders are true to the most well-known advice on the market: buy low and sell high. The ugly part is that most investors do the opposite. They buy when prices have risen out of greed, and they sell out of fear when prices decline. Swing trading is a short-term trading technique that applies the principle of "purchase low and sell big."

Contrary investment in practice is much more complicated than exchange timing. The reverse interprets both fundamental and technical signals in ways that are distinct from common market thought. Timing is only one thing in contrary terms, but it is a critical point for swing traders.

The battle between "the consumer mentality" on the market and the opposite view even applies to theories on which forms of data to be used for decision-making. There is no often disagreement between the basic views (adherence to recent historical financial results as the basis of trade) and the technical views (based on the market action and the trends of predicting the next move or sequence of moves). While swing trade is a strictly technical technique, it can be used in ways that combine both basic and technical indicators. The difference should be clearly understood: choosing individual shares is not the same as timing decisions to buy and sell. In this regard, you may consider selecting a number of stocks you want to trade with using the basics and then use swing trading and other technical tools to delay your decisions.

Investors are too often asked to choose between simple and advanced schools of thought. The use of both makes more sense. Both strategies will narrow your view of what is happening on the market and include flows on both sides. The foundations are purely historical and may be obsolete by the time you decide. Technical indicators are typically short-term, and short-term measures for long-term investment are traditionally unreliable.

What we need to learn from this is that both fundamental and technological aspects can include shortcomings, but both will be useful. Both theories will rely on short-term and long-term trends. The pattern is the secret to selecting stocks and timing decisions for buying and selling.

Day Trading, Long-Term Hold Strategies, and Swing Trading

However, there are several ways to invest in the market, including swing trading, day trading, and long-term holding strategies. However, most conservative investors want low volatility and slow but steady growth; speculators welcome volatile stocks and the unpredictable future, as such stocks show wider price fluctuations. In the light of the unavoidable connection between risk and benefit, a speculator accepts the higher risk. Harm and benefit are, with few exceptions, two sides of the same coin.

Selection of a business considered to be secure is the most conservative position within the market. This means that capitalization is usually high; the company has been in operation for many decades and dominates its market. These businesses have been rising slowly and steadily over the long term. The long-term conservative hold is not exciting but provides a safe, stable foundation for your portfolio.

The highly speculative strategy is on the other side of the risk continuum. People are buying penny stocks, IPOs, and extremely unpredictable issues in this section of the market; trade leverage options and can also combine high-risk commodity business with index portfolios, commodities trading, and commodity future. These are very unusual types of risk, which can only include those who completely understand the business and the risks themselves. To a certain degree, swing traders may want to use alternatives as part of their strategy (see later chapters). However, options can be used in a fairly safe manner to manipulate cash without exposing yourself to massive losses.

This is the difference between the use of instruments such as options by a swing trader and mere speculation. A speculator exposes capital to the risk of loss deliberately, but a swing trader uses options to reduce losses and leverage capital.

The day trader is somewhere between these extremes. This is a trader who actively transfers capital in the extremely short term, usually within a single trading day, into and out of stock. Day traders are typically very voluminous traders, carrying out several regular trades of more than one stock or even of the same stock. If a person buys and sells the same inventory at very high amounts (four times or more in five consecutive days), the Securities and Exchange Commission (SEC) classifies them as a pattern day trader and is subject to similar cash laws that apply to a trading bank.

The swing trader is typically closer to the speculator's side than the conservative investor. This does not necessarily mean that swing trading is high risk relative to other strategies. You can reduce your exposure to capital through swing trading, trade volume, and the number of stocks you trade through minimize the overall risk or restrict your exposure. But everybody should be able to identify where a particular approach belongs in the investment continuum.

In combination with other approaches with different risk characteristics, any approach may also be used. Risk diversification is a wise and effective way to handle your portfolio. For instance, you can use a relatively small portion of your investment capital into your own house, deposit certificates, and Blue Chip stocks and swinging, and other strategies.

The Swing Trade Approach

The exact form of swing trade can differ from person to person. Everyone has their favorite technique type. You know that investors are sometimes clever, often unreasonable, angry, or unrealistically optimistic if you have studied how they behave in the market. The element "what if" is always present.

Swing is a process of creating a set of "rules" that trigger a decision on a trade. It relies on the analysis of stock price trends in the two to five-day window over a short period. Since swing traders agree that short-term price changes represent investor emotions, they trade in a unique way. Instead of selling stocks, swing traders postpone their decisions to match the emotions on the market. This does not mean that the bases of the stock are significant. In fact, the starting point is to narrow a list of stocks, based on fundamental as well as technical analysis, that you swing trade. This may be somewhat contradictory. The aim of using the basics is not to find the best stocks as these are not good swing trading candidates.

The "ideal" stock has solid foundations (excellent management, long-range growth background, etc.) but short-run unpredictable technical signals. That implies, of course, that the trading range is wider than the average stock (the difference between usually high and low prices).

Shift traders, therefore, need well run companies with rather volatile stocks. It is a middle ground; many well-managed businesses are experiencing short-term volatility due to news; the income is uncertain; or product news can cause the stock to rise, fall, or both. So, it is one with solid long-term fundamentals and very unpredictable short-term technical signals if you need to identify the perfect pool of swing trading.

Most investors are not well-informed, and this is where you, as a swing trader, have the benefit. In the atmosphere where greed and fear control decision-making, you match people who are willing to buy inventory from you at a price that is too high; or who are willing to sell stock at a bargain price. You recognize these patterns by tracking daily charts and recognizing turning points, and responding to reverse signals by swing trading. As a swing trader, you profit from other people's impulsive, irrational, and inappropriate decisions.

Most people purchase when they can sell and buy. Swing can be considered a trading technique for emotions (or even for people trading and their propensity to respond with emotions of greed and fear). This implies in some respects that what stocks you exchange does not really matter because the technology applies to all inventories and all short-term fluctuations in the market.

But because stocks are special, the idea to classify a number of stocks according to attributes is still wise, based on

a) Short-term swing trading on the basis of an acceptable level of volatility and
b) Long-term stability is based on stable foundations. This is good advice as other swing traders want to stick with their stocks even though the initial intention was to swing trade. If you actually keep some of the stock you buy, it would be good stock from a long-term point of view.

You detect some very common short-term patterns with the swing trading technology. Though day traders are looking at market fluctuations from time to time, swing traders typically base their timing decision on end-of-day charts. The window for two to five days is focused on the idea that a day's patterns are apparent. The opening and closing rates, the trading range, and the bandwidth (distance from top to bottom) are all relevant for the execution of a swing trade. For example, an opening and closing price and take one day closer to the highest and lowest price levels, and another day could have a slight difference between the opening and closing prices, but show a lot of intermediate action with prices well above and below the actual open and closing price levels.

A swing is a turning point. So, a stock that is rising will swing downwards and vice versa. A swing trader uses open, close, and trading diagram techniques to determine when such swings are most likely to occur. Daily volumes are also critical in the combination of signals that you rely on to build your swing trading strategy.

Within this regular short-term observation of the trend, the direction of price movements every day is also significant. By nature, a swing is most likely when the stock is open and closed in the same direction. This means that the day's closing in an established pattern should be higher than the day opened for at least three consecutive days before the pattern can be relied upon. So when the market trend is down by definition, a downward trend demands that the closing price be lower for at least three days in a row than the opening price. Thus, the overall price range of a day's history is not sufficient; market movement direction must also validate the apparent trend.

The up and downs trend used by swing traders is not the same as the worldwide market patterns. Technicians track market patterns and complex indexes, which are well-known. They also use moving averages of different configurations to signal or predict big ups and downs. The above-mentioned short-term patterns in swing trading are completely different.

This also explains why swing traders frequently stick to the entire pattern of a single trading day. It does not seem to make sense when you first find this rule. A legitimate question might be, 'Will the decision not be made until the patterns of exchange are satisfied instead of at the end of a day? "Every plan will, of course, be as versatile as you need to be. There is no tough and quick requirement that trading takes place only after a day of trading. Nevertheless, swing traders have noticed that the full day is most insightful, even though their timing can be flexible. During a trading day, trends arise based on daytime and the overall direction of the market. For example, many technicians attach great importance to patterns formed in the first hour or two hours. The final hours of trading of a certain stock can be determined primarily by global market trends on the day.

To order to assess the pattern for swing trading, the whole day is treated as the standard, and similarities are therefore consistent. This is also useful in price analysis of any sort. Another significant form of a signal can also be found between the day's closing and the day's opening. Swing traders are likely to play a part, like many other technicians, if the market changes between the two days show wide differences or a high-volume day followed by a low-volume day. Those are examples of the types of changes between days that are considered important to swing traders and also support the idea that you need a full day and not just an hourly shift to building a two or five-day window to recognize a swing trading possibility. A day trader is likely to identify and take advantage of attractive opportunities, but day-trading is a much less complex market practice than swing trading. Although some traders may tend to keep an eye on the stock price throughout the day, swing traders use a more methodical system.

This book describes the exact signs and methods of their observations even more in-depth. The aim here is to give you an overview of how swing trading works and how short-term patterns can be used for benefit.

The basic rule of swing trading is to act after three or more clear signals. When the price is going upward, the signal is to be sold, and when the price is going downward, the signal is to be bought. Keep in mind that the swing is the key. The swing trade theory is based on the premise that short-term price shifts take place at predictable rhythms and cycles. Motion upward in these short-term patterns is accompanied by downward movement and vice versa. To enforce these "rules" of swing trading, several attributes are required. The following are:

1. *Acknowledge a phenomenon*

A real two- to five-day pattern is one in which the markets are opened and closed. In an upward trend, a set of highs will be present per day, along with a range of higher lower ones. Each day's price goes up the top of the day before, and any decline is less than the day before.

2. *Acknowledge a downward trend*

The downward trend also persists over a span of two to five days. It is, however, distinguished by a number of lower and lower heights. Every day's height is lower than the day before, and every day's height is lower than the day before.

3. *Identify an update*

The configuration is a warning that it is time to act. The deployment at the top of the two to a five-day upward trend is a sales warning. And a buy signal is the setup at the end of a two to a five-day downward trend. In other words, the swing trade is based on the premise that these particular signals can be used to assess time and gain from the cyclical price fluctuations.

4. *Look for the narrow day of the selection*

When confirmed, all signals are stronger. The narrow day of trading is a day when the gap from high to low is much less than before "typical trading ranges." If, for example, a share was exchanged in a range of two to three points and there is a two to five (5) day period, a small range day is a clear confirming sign at the end of the cycle. Remember that only after a significant price change is the narrow range day pattern relevant. At the end of a cycle, a typical narrow-range day is a strong buy signal.

5. *Keep an eye on volume changes*

Stocks are typically traded with "typical" regular rates, but changes in this amount also reflect changes in the relationship between buyers and sellers. The unusually high-volume day followed by a narrow-range day is an important cue for swing trading. So when the volume and the width of trade decrease significantly, that indicates that the existing trend is likely to reverse.

These signals should be used in tandem. If there is a two- to five-day uptrend, look for the setup. However, something that is very important in swing trading is confirmation. You have an incredibly powerful buy or sell signal when you can confirm the trend with a setup. The metrics that support this are a narrow day and an improved trading volume. You have incredibly good assurance that it's time to act (to sell after trends or purchase after trends) if you see these two together.

Theory of Chart-Watching

There are two general schools of thinking about how to select stocks and time to buy and sell decisions. The basic school is focused on financial reports and patterns, and pricing is the foundation of the scientific school of thought.

Although both views are worthwhile, it makes sense not to use one or the other, but the two together. Swing is a technological technique, but inventories you choose for swing trade can be selected on the basis of fundamental power. In so far as you rely on technological signals, diagrams are used as the main timing tool. Investors use several different charts, the OHLC chart being the most common. This consists of a vertical line from one day's high to low price and two horizontal tabs. The one to the left is the opening price of the day, and the one to the right is the closing price of the day.

The OHLC chart is common because it offers important details about the operation over a period of time with just three lines. This is reliable. Successful. The point- and figure map is a more abstract map. This involves stacks of Xs and Os irrespective of the time involved. The Xs appear when the price has risen and the Os when the price has fallen. This diagram offers technicians a short overview of trade patterns but is not as easy to use for most investors as the OHLC diagram. Time is generally important for traders to make sound judgments of their stock decisions; the item and figure chart for certain purposes provides a specific type of information but is not so useful as the OHLC. Today's diagramming facilities consist of a changing average and regular price shifts. Besides the essential open, strong, low, and close values, one or more moving average lines are included in the charts. The most famous are averages of 200 days and 50 days. We remove short-term volatility risks and explain how stock markets have developed over time.

The candlestick chart is one last form of chart and one used in future chapters in this book. The descriptive term is given because every day, the trading is white or black, with vertical lines above and below the main body. In Japan in the 18th century, this type of diagram was created to monitor rice prices. U.S. technical analysts and chartists started in the 20th century to recognize the prices of candlesticks to watch OHLC, but also to quickly see if a trend is going up or down.

Both charts outline the flow and trend of short-term and long-term stock price cycles. Price dynamics are inevitably driven by the relationship between consumers and salespeople and a domination of one of the three consumer emotions: greed, fear, and insecurity.

Technicians may see themselves as chartists who rely on particular pricing trends to predict a stock's next direction. The cartographer tends to believe that fundamental analysis has little meaning since it is historical and does not impact the supply and demand forces that control price movement. Some chartists understand that long-term trends are driven by a company's basic strength or weakness but depend on short-term pricing patterns.

There are also pro and con claims about the method of the chartist. On the other hand, the market change trend involves certain predictability. It's not the same as a guarantee, but the price tends to move in a pattern. Swing trading is a common charting technique as it is built for market movement observation and prediction. When prices move in one direction and in a particular manner for three or more trading days, price appears to reverse and then to continue in the opposite direction. Since you cannot know how many times a pattern includes, swing traders try reverse signals to assess their decisions.

Chartists think buyers and sellers connect continuously. If stock prices rise far enough, current owners want to sell for profit, and that leads to a decline in the price. If the price drops far enough, the stock is a sale so that new buyers place orders. The consequence of this interaction is the two to five-day wave action of stocks.

On the flip side, the map just focuses on price and volume, with fundamental news being overlooked by those who monitor the price trend. This is a mistake. For example, following the evolution of stock price trends, a business meets a time limit for releasing a financial report, which is a dangerous signal. In October 2005, for example, Krispy Kreme (the doughnut chain) stocks dropped below USD 6 per share, and the chart may have looked like a buying opportunity for some chartists. Yet something deeper was happening. The company missed its filing date with the SEC, and it was discovered that improper accounting practices were in effect for several years. The stock of the company recovered marginally by the end of 2006 but continued to report quarterly losses. In this situation — where deep fundamental problems were apparent — it would have been a mistake to rely solely on chart patterns.

Chartists do better by mixing simple and technological signals. You may use charts as a primary timing tool for short-term swing-trading; however, a preliminary review of key questions must be carried out for selecting stocks for this play:

- Is the business solvent?
- Has a benefit been registered (more recently or ever)?
- How much debt is the carrying company?
- Is the organization doing well in its field of industry?

You can learn a lot without looking at a financial statement by simply reading the recent titles. Each company receives news online brokerage services. For example, if you are researching Krispy Kreme (KKD) on the brokerage service of Charles Schwab & Company — tps:/investing. Schwab.com — you'll find the stock price, ranking services statistics, comparable prices, and news headlines. The use of both basic and technological knowledge clearly offers quick and reliable information and significantly improves the information base of a chartist.

The Key Emotions: Anxiety, Greed, and Confusion

Chartists who use different tactics are generally focused upon one premise: shorter price fluctuations are often predictable. Some cartographers depend entirely on certain particular pricing trends and tests. Others, like swing traders, claim the three-part emotional pattern controlling how much of the market operates is a pillar of the strategy. While greed, fear, and volatility decide demand trends and make time and market change easier to predict.

Some swing traders describe the strategy as emotional, not inventory-based. But this is not entirely true. A wise trader should also be aware thastocks'e selection is important in a smart system, so that stocks that will behave and respond to normal market forces should be selected. You cannot rely on the usual cyclical trends of short-term mapping so that circumstances that have not given reliable signals, whether you select a depressed stock (such as the Krispy Kreme in 2005) or a stock that is valuable beyond any fundamental reason (such as Amazon.com or eBay in recent times). You will find instructions for choosing swing trade stocks later in this book.

When the selection of possible swing stocks is limited, the timing of trade can be dependent on the three market emotions. Market analysts and financial news media tend to assign names other than raw emotional names to these emotional patterns. When covetousness is in charge, it is called a rally. When fear prevails, and prices begin to fall, correction is called. And when an instability period prevails, this is referred to as a stabilization period.

The phase of acquisition — where there is confusion — is often defined by analysts as an "agreement" time; in other words, both sellers and buyers agree to the current price range. This is false. It is not a time of compromise, but rather of no market control by buyers or sellers. During periods of volatility, the operation to buy and sell needs to be well balanced such that no changes are apparent during supply or demand. There is simply no agreement; both parties have no idea where the stock price will go next.

Another fact is consistent in all three market environments – which is marked by a feeling of greed, fear, and uncertainty: most traders do not learn from past errors. Logically, everyone knows that there is no path forever. If stock price begins to increase, a limit will be set, but covetousness ignores that. As price drops, it can not fall indefinitely, and shares fall to a bargain price level at some point, but fear ignores that fact. So when market volatility (even for just a few days) dominates, traders appear to be impatient. We either lose interest or make an uninformed decision that is at least 50% of the time incorrect. Therefore, investors will sell right in advance, or they will purchase right before prices drop at the end of uncertainty. This is because traders behave impulsively and emotionally. And you should add a fourth emotion with this in mind: impatience. The nervous investor is behaving too hard and making a lot of timing errors.

Swing traders control their emotions and clearly watch how other traders 'emotions communicate with market prices. This contrary approach is more advanced than the standard description. A swing trader is not necessarily purchasing while other people sell and vice versa; the more sophisticated variant includes going against the latest predominant emotion. If prices rise in a whirlwind of greed, the swing merchant finds a sales signal. As prices quickly decrease in the destruction of terror, the swing trader stays calm and finds the indication that the price has fallen. Where confusion is the dominant emotion, swing traders resist the temptation to "do something."

Before analyzing concrete examples from swing trading, you must review the basic principles of technical analysis and interpretation of the charts. The next chapter explores these concepts as a building block to make swing trading an effective market tool.

Trade normally takes time to find out. Maintaining an asset exchange open for a couple of days or weeks could lead to more profitable trading in and out of the same protection many times a day.

CHAPTER 2 : HISTORICAL EVENTS IN THE FX MARKET

It is necessary for any trader to recognize some of the main foreign exchange milestones before moving into the internal functions of monetary trading, as they still present events regularly referenced by experienced forex traders until this very day.

Bretton Woods (1944): Taking the Dollar As The World Currency

Members of 44 nations gathered in Bretton Woods, New Hampshire, in the year after the Second World War in July 1944, creating a new institutional structure to control the international economy. The majority agreed that international financial uncertainty was one of the principal causes of the war and that such instability was one of the main causes of the war. Initially proposed to Great Britain as part of the Lend-Lease Act – which was an American act intended to aid Great Britain in the post-War rebuilding effort – the deal, drawn up by John Maynard Keynes and Harry Dexter White. After several talks, there were some crucial points in the final shape of the Bretton Woods Agreement:

1. The establishment of main international bodies to foster fair trade and economic harmony.

2. Fixing of currency exchange rates.
3. The convertibility of gold and the US dollar, making the US dollar the world's reserve currency.

Of the three parameters described above, only the first point still exists today. The Bretton Woods institutions include the International Monetary Fund (IMF), the World Bank, and the General Tariff and Trade Agreement (GATT), which are all active and have a vital role to play in the growth and control of international economies. For example, the IMF initially implemented the prices of $35 per unit of gold to be established by Bretton Woods, as well as fixing exchange rates during the time of operation of Bretton Woods (and financing necessary to ensure that fixed exchange rates do not create fundamental distortions in the world economy).

The IMF has worked closely with another Bretton Woods progeny since the death of Bretton Woods: the World Bank. Together, the two institutions are now regularly lending funds to developing countries, thereby helping them to build a public infrastructure that can sustain a sound merchant economy that will contribute to the world. The World Bank and the IMF have to co-operate closely with GATT to ensure that these nations will genuinely have equal and legal access to trade with their developed heirs. While GATT originally intended to be a temporary organization, it is now working to promote the elimination of trade barriers – specifically tariffs and quotas.

The Bretton Woods Agreement worked between 1944 and 1971 when the Smithsonian Agreement was replaced by a US groundbreaking international kinds deal. President Richard Nixon out of the need to satisfy the shortcomings of Bretton Woods. The Smithsonian Agreement sadly had the same crucial weakness: while it did not include gold / US. Dollar convertibility, it retained fixed exchange rates — a factor that did not resolve America's current trade deficit and a lower U.S. dollar foreign need. The Smithsonian Agreement was thus short-lived.

Finally, world exchange rates formed into a free market. The only parameters for determining the value of the currency is supply and demand. While this resulted and continues to result in a number of currency crises and increased monetary uncertainty, it also allowed the market to become self-regulatory, and the market can thus determine without obstacles the adequate value of a currency.

As for Bretton Woods, its role in shifting perceptions of the US dollar was perhaps its most memorable contribution to the international arena. While the British pound tends to be considerably stronger, although, for both social activity and foreign exchange, the euro is a disruptive currency forging new boundaries, the US dollar remains the global reserve currency of choice. It is undeniably mainly attributed to the Bretton Woods Accord: the dollar's position as the world's most open and stable currency has been firmly cemented by creating dollar/gold convertibility. Thus, while Bretton Woods may have been a philosophy of the past, it still has its effect on the US dollar and on the international economy.

End Of Bretton Woods - Free Market Capitalism Is Born (1971)

On 15 August 1971, it was formally renovated: the Bretton Woods regime was discarded once and for all. Though exorcized before, this final eradication of the Bretton Woods regime was just the end of its course: currencies could no longer be fixed in gold, just fluctuate within a 1% range, but their rational evaluation could be focused on the free market actions of the currencies including trade flows and foreign direct investment.

Whilst President Nixon was optimistic that the end of the Bretton Woods regime would lead to great moments for the international economy, he was not persuaded that the free market could reasonably and catastrophically determine the true value of the currency. Nixon and most economists concluded that a fully unstructured foreign exchange market would lead to competitive devaluations that would, in effect, break international trade and investment down. Nixon and his economic advisors concluded that the end result would be global depression.

The Smithsonian Agreement was thus adopted a few months later. The Smithsonian Agreement, praised by President Nixon as the "most important monetary agreement in world history," aimed to preserve fixed exchange rates, without gold being sponsored. The biggest difference from the Bretton Woods program was that the value of the dollar was 2.25%, compared to just 1% under Bretton Woods.

In the end, the Smithsonian Agreement also proved impossible. Despite gold fixed exchange rates, the free market price of gold went up to $215 per ounce. In addition, the US trade deficit continued to grow, and from a fundamental point of view, the U.S. dollar had to be devalued beyond 2,25% of the Smithsonian.

Plaza Accord – Devaluation Of Us Dollar (1985)

After all the various exchange rate regulatory arrangements which have defined the gold standard during the 20th century, Bretton Woods remained in a state of deflation. Regrettably, because of a variety of unexpected economic events — such as OPEC, oil crises, stagflation in the 1970s, and dramatic changes in the US. The fiscal policy of the Federal Reserve — supply and demand themselves were inadequate means of controlling the currency markets. A sort system was required, but not an inflexible one. Currency values have been set on a commodity, such as gold, as is also the notion that overall exchange rate fluctuations are fixed.

The balance between stability and rigidity troubled the foreign-exchange markets in the 20th century, and a definite solution was still very necessary as progress was made.

Thus, in 1985, the respective finance ministers and central bank governors of the world's leading economies — France, Germany, Japan, the United Kingdom, and the United States — met in New York City in the hope of reaching a diplomatic agreement of this kind that would maximize the economic efficiency of foreign-exchange markets. World leaders met at the Plaza Hotel and concluded several agreements on individual economies and the global economy as a whole.

Inflation has been very small worldwide. In 1985, the global economy turned 180, in comparison to 1970's stagflation, where inflation was high, and real economic growth was small, with inflation currently low, but growth solid.

While low inflation, combined with strong economic growth, also allows low-interest rates, which are especially appreciated by developing countries, there is an immediate danger of protectionist policies such as the implementation of tariffs into the economy. The US had a large and growing current-account deficit, while Japan and Germany had significant and increasing surpluses. Such a fundamental imbalance, in its essence, could generate a severe economic imbalance, which would, in effect, distort the foreign-exchange markets and thus the international economy.

The consequences of current account imbalances and the resulting protectionist policies warranted intervention. Eventually, the rise of the US dollar, which appreciated over 80% of its major trading partners currencies, was believed to be the key culprit. The increased value of the US dollar led to the development of large trade deficits. On the other side, a dollar with a lower value will be more conducive to stabilizing the international economy because it would inevitably contribute to greater harmony between all countries 'export and import capabilities.

At the Plaza Hotel conference, the United States convinced the other members to arrange the multilateral action, and the Plaza Agreement was adopted on 22 September 1985. This agreement was designed to allow the dollar to decrease and the key anti-dollar currencies to increase controlled. The growing country decided to change its economic policies and, where possible, intervene in the currency markets to may the dollar. The US agreed to reduce its budget deficit and lower interest rates. France, the Netherlands, Germany, and Japan have all agreed to increase interest rates. Germany also agreed to introduce tax cuts while Japan agreed to allow the yen's value to represent the Japanese economy's underlying power. The issue with enforcing the new Plaza agreement, however, was that not all the countries adhered to its commitments. In fact, the United States did not meet its original pledge to cut the budget deficit. As its exporters could not stay competitive overseas, Japan has been badly hurt by the steep yen rise, and it is argued that this ultimately caused a 10-year recession in Japan. As a result of the deal, however, the United States experienced significant development and market stability.

The consequences of the multilateral action were soon noted, and the dollar had fallen by 46% and 50% in the next two years compared with the German mark and the Japanese yen (JPY). The US economy has now been even more export-oriented, while other developed countries such as Germany and Japan have assumed import positions. It increasingly resolved current account deficits at the moment, as well as maintaining limited and non-threatening protectionist policies. But perhaps most significantly, the Plaza agreement cemented the position of the central banks in controlling exchange-rate movements; indeed, the rates were not to be fixed, and thus were to be solely decided by supply and demand; but ultimately, these unseen hands were not sufficient.

George Soros – Man Who Broke The Bank Of England

When George Soros placed a risky $10 billion bet on the UK, Soros was known to be the "man who broke the Bank of England" unanimously. Either you love him or hate him, Soros took over in one of the most interesting incidents in the history of monetary trading.

In 1979, a Franco-German initiative developed a European Monetary System (EMS) to stabilize currencies, minimize inflation, and prepare for monetary integration. The United Kingdom Joins the Exchange Rate Mechanism One of the key components of the EMS, the Exchange Rate Mechanism (ERM), offered every participating currency a central exchange rate for the European Currency Unit (ECU). Participants (initially France, Germany, Italy, the Netherlands, Belgium, Denmark, Ireland, and Luxembourg) then had to keep their exchange rates at or below each central bilateral rate at 2,25% fluctuation. The ERM was an adjustable peg device, with nine modifications between 1979 and 1987. Although the United Kingdom was not one of the initial participants, in 1990, it would finally be replaced by a pound average of 2.95 German marks at + /- 6%.

By mid-1992, the ERM appeared successful, as the punitive effect of the German Bundesbank's leadership has lowered inflation across Europe. The stability would not last, however, as the international investors began to worry about the inadequacy of the exchange rate values of several ERM currencies. AfteGermany'she reunification in 1989, government spending increased, and the Bundesbank was forced to print more currency. This led to higher inflation and left no choice but for the German central bank to increase interest rates. However, the rate increase had more consequences, as it placed upward pressure on the German index. This prompted other central banks also to increase their interest rates in order to preserve the fixed exchange rates (a direct extension of Irving Fisher's principle of interest-rate parity). George Soros knew that the UK's poor economy and the high unemployment rate would not allow the British government to follow this strategy for long.

Soros Bets Against Kingdom Success Participation in ERM

The Quantum Hedge Fund Manager basically wanted to bet the pound depreciated because the UK either devalued the pound or left the ERM. With the gradual abolition of capital controls during EMS years, foreign investors were now more than ever free to benefit from perceived imbalances. Therefore Soros formed short positions in pounds and long-term positions by borrowing and investment in marked assets. He also used options and futures greatly. Together, his positions represented a colossal $10 billion. Not only was Soros, but a lot of other investors were also soon to follow suit. Everyone sold pounds and put massive downward pressure on the currency.

At first, by purchasing 15 billion pounds with its huge reserves, the Bank of England attempted to protect the tied prices, but its sterilized interventions (which have a constant monetary basis thanks to free-market interventions) were limited in their effectiveness. The pound traded dangerously near the lower end of its set band. On 16 September 1992, which later would be dubbed Black Wednesday, the bank reported a 2% rise in interest rates from 10% to 12% in an effort to raise the appeal for the pound. It agreed to increase prices again to 15% a few hours later, but foreign investors such as Soros could not be swayed because enormous profits are just around the corner. Traders continued to sell pounds to large amounts, and the Bank of

England continued to buy pounds until 7 p.m. Around the same day, Chancellor Norman Lamont announced that Britain would exit the ERM, restoring the levels to their original 10% level. The tumultuous Black Wednesday marked the start of a sharp decline of the productive value of the pound.

It remains today to be debated whether the return to a floating currency was the result of the Soros-led attack on a pound or simply a fundamental analysis. Yet what is clear is that the almost 15% fall of the pound against the German market and 25% against the dollar over the next five weeks contributed to huge profits for Soros and other traders. The Quantum Fund invested around $2 billion within a month by selling the still most costly German marks and buying back the still cheaper pounds. "The guy who broke the British Bank" revealed how central banks would still be vulnerable to speculation.

Asian Financial Crisis (1997–1998)

On 2 July 1997, the relatively new Asian tiger economies set a perfect example in illustrating global capital markets 'interdependence and subsequent impacts in foreign currency forums. Depending on many structural breakdowns, the cause of infection has been mainly caused by overcrowded credit, inflationary trade deficits, and weak capital markets. In addition, the variables led to a "perfect storm" that left large global markets incapacitated and once-priced currencies substantially lower. With adverse effects in stock markets easily seen, currency fluctuations were negatively affected during this time.

The Bubble

Until 1997, the Bubble Leading attracted investors gradually to Asia's investment opportunities, concentrating on immovable and domestic equities. Foreign investment capital has thus poured into the region as growth levels have risen in improved production in countries such as Malaysia, the Philippines, Indonesia, and South Korea. Thailand, home to the baht, had a 13% growth rate in 1988 (fallen to 6.5% in 1996). The creation of a fixed currency binding to the dominant US dollar offered additional lending support for a stronger economy. With a steady greenback assessment, countries like Thailand could ensure financial stability in their own markets and a consistent export trade rate with the largest economy worldwide. Ultimately, domestic currencies in the area were priced as underlying fundamentals, and speculative positions were justified in expectation of further price climbs.

Non-performing Loans and Ballooning Current Account

Nevertheless, in early 1997, a change in sentiment had begun, as foreign account deficits were becoming increasingly difficult for each government to cope with, and credit practices had been shown to be detrimental to the financial infrastructure. Economists were especially warned that Thailand's current account deficit had ballooned to $14.7 billion in 1996. While comparatively smaller than the United States deficit, the difference accounted for 8 percent of the country's gross domestic product. Different lending practices have also made a major contribution to these breakdowns, as strong personal ties between lenders and high-ranking bank officials have been well-paid and shockingly popular across the country. In this way, many heavily leveraged conglomerates in South Korea have been affected as the overall non-performing loan values increased to 7.5% of the gross domestic product.

There may be more evidence of these activities in financial institutions across Japan. Following the disclosure of a total of $136 billion in questionable and non-performing loans in 1994, Japanese officials acknowledged an unprecedented amount of $400 billion a year later. In addition to a subsequently collapsing stock market, refreshing real estate prices, and dramatic economic downturns, investors saw a depreciative yen as a way of applying sales leverage to neighboring currencies. When Japan's asset bubble burst, asset prices dropped by $10 trillion, with immobilization falling by almost 65 percent of the overall two-year decrease. This collapse in asset prices sparked the Japanese banking crisis. It started in the early 90s and in 1997, after the collapse of many prominent financial institutions, grew into a full-blown systemic crisis. As a result, Japanese monetary authorities have cautioned against increasing benchmark interest rates in the hope of upholding the national currency assessment. Unfortunately, these factors have never materialized, and a deficit has resulted. Driven largely by an advertisement of the Thai Baht's managed float, the slide blasted as the central Bank reserves evaporated and the level of monetary prices became unsustainable due to a downside selling pressure.

Currency Crisis

The aforementioned Asian economies were left devastated and temporarily incapacitated after widespread short speculation and attempted intervention. Thailand baht, once a cherished currency, has been devalued by as much as 48%, dropping closer to 100% at New Year's turn. The Indonesian rupiah was the worst affected. Relatively stable before the start of the Thai Baht "crawl," the Rupiah fell to the U.S. dollar, a whopping 228% of its previous high of 12,950. Amongst the big yen, the Japanese yen dropped from its peak to its low in 1997 and 1998 to around 23 percent relative to the United States dollar.

The 1997-1998 financial crisis exposed the interconnectivity and impact of economies on global currency markets. Moreover, central banks were unable to effectively interfere in currency valuations in the absence of stable economic fundamentals as compared with overwhelming market powers. Today, Asia's four dragons are churning again with the aid of IMF repair packages and the introduction of tougher specifications. Southeast Asia is restoring its once-influential status among developed economic areas in the world with inflationary expectations and a revived export market. With the experience of evaporating currency reserves, Asian tigers are now taking active measures to ensure that they have a large stockpile available in the event that speculators are attempting to once again strike their currencies.

The introduction of the euro was quite a monumental achievement that marked the largest monetary changeover ever. January 1st, 1999, the Euro was officially launched as an electronic trading currency. Belgium, Germany, Spain, France, Ireland, Italy, Luxembourg, the Netherlands, Austria, Portugal, and Finland are among the 11 original members of the European Monetary Union (EMU). Two years later, Greece left. -- country set its currency against the euro, and it adopted a common monetary policy controlled by the European Central Bank (ECB). The scheme would potentially encompass all of the original 15 members of the European Union (EU) for several economists, but the United Kingdom, Sweden, and Denmark preferred to retain their own currencies for now. The circulation of Euro notes and coins started only in the first two months of 2002 when determining whether to accept the euro, the pros and cons of such a significant decision had to be weighed by all EU leaders.

Although easy travel is perhaps the biggest issue for EMU people, the Euro also has many other advantages:

- It prevents exchange-rate volatility, thus providing a more stable environment for trade in the euro area.
- The absence of any exchange rate risk in the region helps businesses to make investment decisions with greater certainty.
- Reduced transaction costs (mostly those related to foreign exchange trades, hedging, cross-border payments, and multi-currency account management).
- Markets are becoming more transparent as customers and businesses can compare prices more easily across countries. In addition, this increases competition.
- For international investors, the vast single currency market is becoming more attractive.
- The reach and stability of the economy allow the ECB, thanks to increased credibility, to manage inflation at lower interest rates.

However, the euro is not infinite. Apart from political autonomy, the major problem is that a country primarily forfeits its autonomous monetary policy with the adoption of the euro. Since the economy of each country is not entirely linked to the economy of the EMU, during a domestic recession, a nation may consider the ECB higher interest rates. This refers, in particular, too many smaller nations. As a result, countries are attempting to rely more heavily on fiscal policy, but fiscal policy effectiveness is limited when not effectively paired with monetary policy. This inefficiency is compounded by the budgetary deficit cap of 3% of GDP, as provided for in the Stability and Growth Pact.

There are some questions about the efficacy of the ECB as a central bank. While its target inflation is slightly below 2%, inflation in the eurozone rose above the threshold in 2000-2002 and was late in surpassing the self-imposed goal. From 1999 to the end of 2002, a lack of confidence in the Union's currency (and in the union itself) triggered a decline of 24% from about $1.15 per dollar in January 1999 to around $0.88 per year in May 2000, which in the last few months of 2000 forced the ECB to intervene on foreign exchange markets. Since then, things have changed greatly; the euro is now trading premium to the dollar, and many experts predict that soon the euro will replace the dollar as the world's main foreign currency.

Ten more participants are expected to join the euro in the next few years. The enlargement, with the EMU population increasing by one quarter, is both politically and economically a significant event: all but two immigrants, after 15 years of transition, are former Soviet republics and join the EU. When assimilated, these countries would become part of a community of 450 million citizens, one of the world's largest free trade zones. Therefore, Poland, Hungary, and the Czech Republic, which account for 79 percent of the new member GDP combined, are not expected to accept the euro any long. While euro members are required to reduce fiscal deficits by 3% of GDP, each of these countries currently has a deficit estimated to be about 6%. In a possible scenario, the entry of the euro into Poland, Hungary, and the Czech Republic is possible to be postponed as early as 2009. And smaller countries whose economies currently meet EU criteria face a long replacement cycle for their national currencies. States which are already keeping a fixed euro exchange rate – Estonia and Lithuania – could participate in the ERM sooner but would still be able to adopt the euro on a fairly fast track until 2007.

The Maastricht Treaty of 1993 laid down five key convergence conditions for membership of the EMU.

Treaty of Maastricht: Compatibility Requirements

1. The government budget deficit of the country does not exceed 3 percent of GDP.
2. The government debt of the nation does not exceed 60 percent of GDP.
3. For two years before joining, the exchange rate of the country had to be held within ERM bands without any realignment.
4. The inflation rate of the country cannot be higher than 1.5 percent above the three EU countries with the lowest inflation levels.
5. The country's long-term interest rate on government bonds should not be higher than 2% of the equivalent rates in the three lowest inflation countries.

CHAPTER 3 : BASIC TECHNICAL RULES

Mostly price related to the methods used in technical analysis. They are, in fact, visual. Technicians give great weight to trade and price trends. The fundamental analysis is, by comparison, an empirical study using financial results to determine recent trends and to predict future value — and thus, growth in prices. Although basic analysis looks backward, technical analysis is aimed at forecasting future trends in prices. Investors may effectively use these two strategies to enhance risk detection, stock selection, and timing:

1. *Risk detection*

When people hear about risk, they just think of the risk of losing money versus making money. This is market risk, and every stock investor continually faces this risk. Nevertheless, the definition of this danger is difficult since so many facets of the company and the stock must be taken into account.

Technical analysis involves price and volatility comparisons, which are another dimension of market risk. The perfect swing stock is one with volatility rates. Price swings are necessary to achieve the required variance in swing trading so that a very low volatility stock is not working. On the other hand, highly volatile inventories are unstable and not ideal for most swing trading operations. Based on market risk, the most appropriate stocks are those that are moderately volatile and that trade within a range of more than just a few trading points.

2. *Selection of stock*

Of course, choosing stocks is the deciding move in making a profit or sustaining losses. Investors prefer to use stock selection approaches based on basic technical signals, but they are always incorrect. For instance, some people buy a stock because the price has recently risen, or they sell their shares because the price has fallen. A logical approach for selecting stocks may include fundamental analysis and a detailed review of the key financial ratios and patterns, and the technical analysis for the timing of businesses that involve swing trading.

3. *Decision timing*

Basic research is based on past financial results — and this is an issue. The business is evolving from time to time. Technicians correctly claim that fundamental analyzes can not be used for trade timing. Although the basics can and should be used to pick stocks, you must use technical signals to ensure that the buying and selling decisions are properly timed. To this end, Swing trading is a valuable tool.

Resistance and Support

A stock's trading range is the price area where the stock is bought and sold. This range defines what is "natural" so that when stock prices move above or below that range – or even if the price checks take place on the edges of the range – such events are important. In short, technological research functions like this. It is about defining and recognizing certain laws and determining what it means when the stock price violates those rules.

The trading range will take various forms. The most simple is price-based so that trading is stationary. The price above and below does not adjust. A second category is the changing set of markets in which the size stays approximately the same, but the price rate increases or falls. Figure 2.1 demonstrates these three types of trading ranges.

When a trading range grows, technicians call this pattern parallel price channels and are usually seen to pre-empt a transition in the trading sector in the immediate future. The degree and speed of a changing trade range, called a momentum phenomenon, is also critical in deciding how and when the trading range will change in the future.

The trading range is often characterized by high and low prices. If a stock is within a given range of trading, these lines will continue intact. However, if the price crosses these price lines, there will be major changes, and a new trading range will be created.

The resistance point is the top line of the trading scale. This is the highest price traders prepared to pay for the stock. The lowest price sellers can agree to give up stock is the support level. The support and resistance lines provide a clear, price based description of the current stock supply and demand level in the ongoing relationship between buyers and sellers.

The foundations of technical analysis are resistance and support. They provide the benchmark by which the output of a stock is assessed in many respects. The following criteria include:

1. *The distribution and thus the stock volatility*

The higher the price swing from high to low within the exchange range, the higher the uncertainty. The most common indicator of market risk is high volatility, so the technician assesses stock protection on the basis of its spread.

2. *The pattern is flat, up or down*

The tendency can be flat or changing, helping to define the stock too. Swing traders are reliant on a degree of volatility, or the strategy just won't work; most short-term traders would accept that they need some price changes to execute their trading strategies. This is a problem for the short term. The long-term price performance of a stock relies on the intensity of the fundamental principles of the company; short-term price performance is controlled by consumer emotions, and moderate volatility is beneficial.

3. To what extent the trade spectrum limits are checked, and what these checks entail

Technicians characterize price movement as if the price itself was conscious. Therefore they describe a price pattern as "aggressive" or "indecisive" because technicians claim that when prices reach resistance or support thresholds, they "matched" these limits. A test that does not succeed usually shows that the price will shift in the other direction; when the price breaks down, it is seen as an important development that puts the existing trade portfolio in total disorder and often leads to the creation of a new trade portfolio. Many technicians such as military analogies, a price breakthrough is thus defined as a military breakthrough. This causes confusion and chaos and can lead to a catastrophe (or in the case of trade, to a new resistance or help "front line").

4. Present shifts in the range as values are above or below set boundaries

When a breakthrough is made, there is often a period of uncertainty after which a new trading range is created. That is inevitable. Stock prices cannot be expected to remain forever within a small trading range, as new changes in a trading range and volatility rates are part of the life cycle of a stock. From the point of view of technicians, the modifications are viewed on the basis of price-fixing. The new trading range may be more volatile or less volatile than the previous one. The formerly set selection can be replaced by a changing one. The price differences between periods are the important features of technical analysis. The unpredictability of price trends can be resolved by correctly analyzing the signals from a technical point of view.

5. *The implications when a stock is so unpredictable that a trading range cannot be calculated*

In some situations, the stock price is so erratic that no clear trading range for the short term can be defined. The price is completely unpredictable. This poses a dilemma for everybody because there is no clear definition. The instability is due to some important market uncertainty, but rather than a smooth, short-term price setting, it becomes wildly unpredictable. This pattern is always short-term and triggered by a question or perception moving through. A shrewd technical analyst knows that an analysis of the underlying causes will help to predict the duration of the high volatility.

Studying resistance and support and how prices operate within the trading range is important for swing traders as it lets you predict market action in the next 3-5 days. While you can rely on the graph patterns and signals mentioned in the following three chapters, be aware of the range of trading. It represents the premise of stock risk, price actions, and future trends that have not yet fully formed.

The Benefits of Short-Term Chaos

Trading adds a certain amount to an otherwise unpredictable situation. Nobody knows what the stock price will next do, just as nobody can forecast the financial market accurately. The auction system where stock trading happens is volatile since so many opposing powers and interests are involved. An economic model addresses supply and demand as if buyers and sellers work on a particular basis. Offering and demand are very different in practice.

Since supply and demand are dynamic forces operating at several different rates, prices never shift permanently in one direction. As stock prices rise, other owners take advantage and sell. The more shares are sold, the lower the rates. This is an ongoing exchange. It also has an impact in purchasing or selling stock blocks in a single move by major institutional investors, such as the mutual funds, insurance firms, and pension plan managers.

The investor, also known as the retail investor, is just a small proportion of the overall volume of trading. It does not mean that people have no influence over the economy. Institutional investors continue to make the same mistakes as individuals; deal with short-term emotions instead of logic, and misread market signals. That is how you would profit from swing trading. Institutions are too complicated and have too many stocks in their portfolios to determine quickly; you should, as a single person, move rapidly on and off the waves of short-term prices shift.

Short-term uncertainty is the benefit of retail investors. Since your concern is a small number of stocks and a very short time span, you can make quick decisions and yet bear low trading costs. As the short-term trend is often volatile and driven by covetousness, fear, and insecurity, one thing you can constantly expect: prices will overreact to any news. If the profit of a stock is a few cents below analysts 'expectation, the stock can fall much more than the news warrants (only in a matter of days to change to a better level). This is, of course, a swing trading chance. You should also note that the Chaos Period – the time span during which overreaction is regulated in any direction – takes 3 to 5 days. Therefore, swing trading works well on the same timetable. It takes three to five days for buyers and sellers to identify the price overreaction and the change to be resolved. In addition, the time that institutional investors have to correct their stock positions (represented by large stocks) prevents them from acting more quickly. The downside for institutional investors is the greatest gain for individual swing traders.

You can forecast how rates will change in the short term in this regard. There must be a distinction between short-term demand movements and longer-term industry patterns. Under the auspices of the Dow Theory developed by Dow Jones 'co-founder

Charles Dow, the key technological framework on the market operates. A hundred years ago.

Dow was conscious that patterns are the secret to predicting potential market patterns. Dow theory has become a set of rules and observations, as its ideas have been refined over the years, usually applied in the whole sector and embodied by Dow Jones Industrials and others.

The Dow Theory states that many developments can be seen in the broader market. A long-term trend, after an index was developed and then verified by another, sets the direction of the market. In the Dow Theory, however, short-term patterns are dismissed as unreliable.

That's real. When you think about long-term patterns for the entire industry, you can't rely on a price change of 2 to 5 days. More time is required to create a long-term primary or secondary pattern. Yet swing traders don't bother with these patterns. The short-term pattern that a swing trader follows is the over-reaction on the market to nearly all news and all changes within the business and the individual stock. In that regard, swing traders observe and take decisions based on the movements generated by greed, fear, and insecurity. You can pick stocks based on long-term growth and basic energy, but trade in emotions and not basics. It is where you can use short-term uncertainty to maximize your gain.

Trading Ranges Breakouts

Short-term price fluctuations in a trading range can be considered negligible. It makes sense from a long-term point of view, considering the truth. To order to predict long-term growth, short-term patterns cannot be relied on. Fundamental observers should universally agree with this. But short-term trading cycles are driven by greed and fear, and that is the secret to swinging trade success. Even technical experts agree.

When prices change in emotional reaction, they are often inflated. A greed-driven price increase will thus surpass all rational or justified stock price rises, and anxious price declines will also go beyond a reasonable or justified stage. Swing traders rely on emotions in this respect and don't spend time studying the underlying causes of price movement. This is important not because price cycles respond to no underlying cause but because these emotions are guided.

This is a really fast price change. Swing traders can also be fundamental analysts, so you may play both positions unless you combine the two separate thinking schools. But it is time for the price to push beyond resistance or below help. This may occur if greed and fear are so exaggerated that panic takes over, in which case, the price will eventually return to the existing trading range. This is the exception: a break-up is more likely because the stock price is on the way to a new trading range.

A breakdown happens in several different forms and follows some particular maps. Chartists use some of these trends to forecast an outbreak. Sometimes it is hard to interpret a current chart pattern correctly, but it is easier to detect in retrospect.

A collapse can be more drastic than the examples shown, with rates well above or below set levels. A relatively low volatility stock can only become highly volatile for a period of time and become a new trade range at a different level than previously defined. When you imagine a long-range stock chart, over months and years, you can see the general trends, and moving averages are useful for assessing those trends. But, if only for a short period of time, changes in stock price rates can be very unpredictable, and new trading opportunities can be created.

Another significant pattern of trade is distance. As a general rule, stocks tend to open a new day within the previous day's high-low boundaries. The gap, also known as the common gap, is not uncommon. When a stock price opens above or below its low point in the previous day, there is a gap; and depending on the subsequent market operation, a gap can exist in various forms.

The breakaway gap entails price movement into a range in which it was not in the last few years, a "breakaway" from the previously established trading range. In contrast, the typical difference is within a fixed range of trade.

For technicians, two other types of gaps are significant. The first is the fatigue gap, which occurs after a long period of upward or downward price movement. Although the exhaust gap continues in the same direction, it suggests that the price trend may end and the price trend reversed. A flat gap is created when the price movement gains strength; this kind of gap reinforces the price trend, and a series of flat gaps can even occur one at a time.

Because of what they sometimes mean, gaps are relevant for swing traders; gaps follow significant changes in the paths at the start of new price movements and also at the end of the same patterns. If you look at charts and see trends that suggest the timing is right, then a validation form will validate your decision and boost your time frame. Laps are one of the best types of confirmation for entering or exiting a company.

Essential Chart Patterns

As a swing trader, you don't have to become an expert in technical analysis in all ways – and some of it is very complicated. However, the simple charts need to be mastered, and these are fairly fast.

Two general levels of technical analysis are available. The biggest and most complex is also overly abstract and mathematical. This level is more theoretical than real and is typically taught to students. When you complete this report, the stock has moved to its next stage, and the information is out of date. A few critical fundamentals are at a more immediate and open level. You will quickly acquire the information needed to boost your timing and income with swing trading.

The most well-known signs are double-top and double-bottom patterns and are very basic indications to be seen and interpreted. Two resistance checks require a double top with a decrease in the price between them. As a result of the sole reason that this is a double check, the double top signal is considered to be bullish, and the inventory price should withdraw. The argument here is that buyers have not been optimistic enough to drive the price higher. On the opposite, the double bottom is a help check. If the support is powerful enough for this two-part check, then the price increases.

The pattern of the head and shell is an extended variation on the top or bottom of the double pattern. This is characterized by three price peaks or decreases, the middle one going beyond the first and the third (in M form letter). At or close resistance occurs a head and shoulder top; Intermediate trade areas between peaks are known as the neckline of the pattern. At the first "shoulder," the volume is always high and at the final step of the design fairly low. The head-and-shoulders top is a resistance measure and anticipates a price decrease as it does not crack.

The bottom head and shoulder tests endorse the same resistance as the top tests but in the opposite direction in letter type W. The amount of the last of three head-and-should extensions is probably lower than for the first shoulders and the reverse back, suggesting that investors are not very optimistic about a decline in rates. The bottom of the head and shoulders anticipates a rise in the stock price.

The two head-and-shoulders model each of the predicted price changes in the opposite direction of the tests and can also predict breaks from the specified trading range (under help following the top pattern and above stamina following the bottom pattern).

Partnership. In the light of these problems, in February 1972, the foreign exchange markets had to close.

The forex markets reopened in March 1973 but were not bound by a Smithsonian Agreement: the US dollar's value was decided entirely by the market because no commodity's value was set, nor was the fluctuation of its exchange rate limited to certain parameters. While this provided by necessity, the U.S. dollar, and other currencies, it also set the stage for unprecedented inflation in order to adjust to the current and rapidly changing foreign trade conditions. The end of the Smithsonian and Bretton Woods Agreement and the Middle East conflict, which led to significantly higher oil prices, helped stagflation the U.S. economy — the combination of unemployment and inflation. The US dollar would return to usual expectations no later than the decade, as the Federal Reserve Chairman Paul Volcker unveiled new economic policies. President Ronald Reagan introduced a new fiscal policy. At that time, foreign exchange markets had fully evolved and could now serve a multitude of purposes: they started to draw speculators seeking to engage in a market with unequaled liquidity and continued development while implementing a laissez-faire model of regulation in international trade. In the end, the demise of Bretton Woods in 1971 signaled the start of a new economic age, which opened up foreign markets and proliferated investment opportunities.

CHAPTER 4 : FUNDAMENTAL TRADING STRATIGIES

Many traders fail in forming perceptions around a single currency without taking account of the relative strength and weakness of both currencies in the pair they sell. This ignorance of the external economic conditions in the FX market is likely to significantly prevent a trade's profitability. It also increases the risk of failure. There is more room for failure when trading against a strong economy; the currency you want to trading could fluff badly, forcing you to stick to a currency more likely to appreciate. Similarly, there is an increased risk that the other currency will improve and result in marginal profits in trade. Finding strong economic/weak economic combinations is also a successful tactic to use when attempting to optimize returns.

Take, for instance, 22 March 2005 – the United States. In its Federal Open Market Committee (FOMC), Federal Reserve raised its inflation risk, causing any major currency pair to tank against the dollar. In addition, a range of strong US economic data further boosted the power of the dollar. While you could have won a long dollar trade at that point, the dollar appreciation in some pairs was much greater than in others. For instance, in the weeks after the first bloodbath, the pound showed a turnaround, while the yen depreciated for a long time. The explanation was that at this time, Britain's economy displayed a steady, impressive amount of economic growth that helped it reclaim significant ground in a matter of weeks after the compulsive dollar hysteria. For the British pound, there was a recovery against the dollar. After a low of 1,8595 on the 28th of March, the pair resumed their pre-FOMC stage of 1,9200 in the next three weeks.

On the other hand, the Japanese yen endured a decline in the USD / JPY pair well into the middle of April for a long time. The dollar improved another 300 pipes over the next two weeks following the FOMC meeting. One cause of discrepancies in these movements was the lack of confidence among market watchers in the Japanese economy, which was on the brink of recession and showing no clear signs of economic growth. Thus, the dollar strength had a much higher impact and higher stamina with the fighting yen than with the reliably powerful pound.

Naturally, interest rates and other geopolitical macro-events are also significant but finding the best economic strength and the weak economy pairing can lead to higher chances of success when comparing two equally compelling trades. Examining crosses of the major companies during this time span reveals another way to maximize productivity by understanding the strengths of various currency pairings.

After the 22 March FOMC conference, AUD / JPY and EUR / JPY were both sold out, but JPY / AUD bound up much faster than EUR / JPY. One of the reasons for this could very well be the clear contrast between the economy and the weak economy. In 2003, 2004, and 2005, the Eurozone economy experienced very slow inflation. On the other side, Australia performed much better, with Australia providing one of the highest interest rates in the industrialized world in the first half of 2005 and throughout 2004. The currency pair thus bounced back considerably faster than EUR / JPY post FOMC. That is why it is important to bear in mind strong economic/weak economic pairings when searching for a trade.

LEVERAGED CARRY TRADE

The leveraged transportation strategy is one of the global macro hedge fund and investment banks 'favorite trading strategies. It is the largest global macro exchange. In short, the trading technique involves long or high- currencies and the selling or shortening of low- currency. Aggressive speculators leave the exchange rate risk unregulated, meaning the speculator bets that in addition to receiving the interest rate gap between the two currencies, the high rating currency would appreciate. For those who cover the exposure to exchange rates, while interest rates appear to be fairly small, the gains from the interest rates may, by themselves, be significant in the scale 1 to 5 percent, if the traders have a 5 to 10 times leverage factor. Only think: A 2.5% interest rate gap is 25% on 10 times the leverage. If not properly managed, leverage can also be very dangerous because it can aggravate losses. The accumulation of capital generally occurs when several traders see this potential and also pile up into the exchange that eventually brings the currency pair together.

In foreign exchange trading, transportation is a simple way to benefit from this fundamental economic theory that money continuously enters and flows away from different markets, guided by the economic laws of supply and demand: the markets with the highest returns on investments usually draw the most capital. Countries are no different in the world of international capital flows; countries with the highest interest rates can usually draw the most investment and generate the highest currency demand. A very common trading strategy, trading is easy to handle. When done properly, the return can be high without an investor taking a lot of risks. However, carriage trades have some risk. There are great chances of failure if you don't understand how, why, and when trades work best.

How Does Carry Trade Works?

As a carrying business works, a currency is bought that provides a high-interest rate when selling a low-interest-rate currency. Carrying transactions are lucrative because an investor will gain the difference in interest rates or spread between the two currencies. Example: Assume the Australian dollar offers a 4.75 percent interest rate while the Swiss franc offers a 0.25 percent interest rate. An investor buys the Australian dollar to carry out the exchange and sells the Swiss franc. It may make a profit of 4.5% in that case, unless the exchange rate between Australian dollars and Swiss francs shifts, which is 4.75% in the interest earned minus 0.25% in the interest paid. This return is based on a leverage of zero. Five-fold leverage yields a return of 22.5 percent on the interest rate gap. See the example below and Figure 10.5 to explain how an investor can actually make the carriage trade:

Carrying out the Carry Trade

Buying AUD and sell CHF (long AUD / CHF).

Place long AUD: an investor gains 4.75%.

Short position CHF: investor pays 0.25%.

With a constant spot rate, profits are 4.50 or 450 basis points.

If the currency pair both increased value because other traders noticed this opportunity, the carrier would gain not only return but also capital appreciation.

In summary: A transaction is carried through the purchase of a currency that offers a high-interest rate in the cause of selling a currency with a low-interest rate.

Why Do This Trade Work?

Act on trade because capital flows continuously in and out of countries. Interest rates are a great reason why, as opposed to others, some countries draw more investment. If a country's economy does well (high growth, high productivity, low unemployment, rising incomes ...), it can offer higher returns on investments to those investing in the country. Another way of saying this is to suggest that countries with better prospects of development can afford to offer a higher interest rate on their money invested.

Investors tend to receive higher interest rates, so investors would obviously look for investments that give them the highest return rate. They want to maximize their income. In case an investor decides to invest in a particular currency, the investor is more likely to choose the one with the highest rates of return or interest. When several investors decide exactly the same, the country will experience a capital inflow from those who are searching for a high rate of return.

What about countries that economically don't do well? Countries with low growth and low productivity can not give investors a high return on investment. In fact, some countries have such poor economies that they can not give any return on investments, which means that the interest rates are zero or close.

This difference between high-interest rates countries and low-interest rates makes carriage trades possible.

Let's look at the previous example, but slightly more detailed: imagine an investor in Switzerland that earns a yearly interest rate of 0.25% on its Swiss francs bank deposit. At the same time, a bank in Australia gives an Australian dollar deposit of 4.75 percent a year. As the interest rates of the Australian bank are much higher, the investor would like to find a way to earn that higher interest rate on its assets.

Now imagine that the investor will exchange his Swiss franc deposit paying 0.25 percent for a 4.75 percent Australian dollar deposit. She has basically sold her Swiss franc deposit and bought an Australian dollar deposit. After this investment, she now owns a dollar deposit from Australia, which charges her 4.75% of the interest per year, 4.50% higher than her Swiss franc deposit.

Basically, the investor has recently made trade by "purchasing" a deposit of the Australian dollar and by "selling" a deposit of the Swiss franc.

The net impact of the exchange is that capital flows out of Switzerland and into Australia as investors take Swiss francs and swap them for Australian dollars. Australia can draw more money because of its higher rates. This capital inflow raises currency value.

To summarize: the gap in interest rates between countries makes carry trades. Investors are looking to buy and hold high interest-rate currency as they want to gain higher interest rates.

When Does Carry Trade Work Best?

During certain times, carry-trades work better than others. In fact, transportation is the most profitable when investors as a group have a very specific risk attitude.

How many chances do you want to take? People's moods may change over time, and sometimes they may feel more bold and willing to take the opportunity, while others may be shier and prone to conservative behavior. As a group, investors are no different. They are sometimes willing to make investments involving a good deal of risk; others are afraid of losses and look forward to investing in safer properties.

In financial jargon, when investors are willing to take risks as a whole, we mean that they are at low risk or are in risk-seeking mode. In comparison, we claim they have a high risk tolerance as investors are attracted to more conservative investments and are less willing to thigh-risk.

Trade carriers are the most attractive for low-risk investors. This argument makes sense when you consider what a transportation trade is about. To recap, a carrying company requires the buying of a denomination with a high-interest rate then it selling it at a currency with a low-interest rate. The investor is risky in purchasing the high-interest rates currency – it is quite unclear whether the country's economy can continue to operate well and be able to pay high rates of interest. In fact, there is a clear chance that something could happen that prevents the country from paying this high rate. In the end, the investor must be willing to take this opportunity.

If the investors as a whole were not willing to take that risk, capital would never pass from one country to another, and there would be no trading opportunity. To be able to work, transactions either allow investors as a group to have a low-risk tolerance or to take the risks of investing in the currency that has a higher interest rate.

In short, transactions have the greatest profit potential in periods when investors are willing to risk investing in high interest-paying currencies.

When Won't Carry Trades Work?

So far, we have shown that transportation works best if investors have a low aversion to risk. What happens if high-risk aversion occurs to investors?

Trades in carrying are the least competitive if buyers are very aggressive. If investors have a high-risk aversion, as a group, they are less likely to take their investment opportunities. They will also be less likely to invest in more volatile currencies with higher interest rates. Rather, if investors are extremely aggressive, they would prefer to put their money in "safe haven" currencies that pay lower interest rates. That would be the exact opposite of a transportation company — in other words, buyers purchase the low-interest rate of the currency and sell the currency at a high-interest rate.

Returning to our earlier example, if the investor suddenly feels insecure keeping the Australian dollar as a foreign currency. Now she is more interested in keeping her investment secure instead of searching for a higher interest rate. In this way, she exchanges her Australian dollars for Swiss francs that are more common.

The net result of millions of transactions is that investors obtain Australian dollars from Australia and Switzerland and exchange them for Swiss francs. Because of this high-risk aversion of investors, Switzerland attracts more money, despite the lower interest rates, because its currency provides stability. This capital inflow raises the Swiss franc value.

To sum up: transportation would be the least lucrative when investors do not wish to take the risk of investing in high-interest paying currencies.

The Benefit of Risk Aversion

Bring companies are typically profitable if investors have low-risk aversions and are unprofitable if investors are at high risk. However, it is therefore imperative to be aware of the risk climate before putting a transportation company – if investors as a whole have high- or low-risk aversions – and when they shift.

Increased risk aversion is usually advantageous for low interest-rate-paid currencies. Investors 'moods change quickly at times — investors' ability to make risky trades will radically change from moment to moment. Such big changes are also triggered by major global events. Where investor risk aversion increases rapidly, the result is typically a large influx of capital into low-income "safe haven" currencies. In the summer of 1998, for instance, the Japanese yen appreciated more than 20 percent against the dollar over the period, primarily due to the Russian debt crisis and the rescue of long-term capital management hedge funds. Likewise, just after the 11 September 2001 terrorist attacks, over a 10-day period, the Swiss franc increased more than 7 percent relative to the dollar.

These fast currency fluctuations also occur when the risk aversion switches rapidly from low to high. As a result, a carrier trade can also rapidly turn from profitable to unprofitable if risk tolerance shifts in this way. Conversely, with an aversion to the risk of creditors from large to low, transportation is more competitive.

How do you know that investors in their entirety have a high or low-risk aversion? Unfortunately, average investor risk is difficult to calculate with a single number. One way to get a general understanding of the extent of risk tolerance is to look at the various returns bonds pay. The wider the gap, or spread, between credit rating bonds, the greater the investor's risk aversion. In most financial newspapers, bond returns can be found. However, many large banks have built their own risk aversion mechanisms that show when and when investors are willing to take risks.

Other Things to Consider When Looking at a Carry Trade

While risk aversion is no doubt one of the most vital things to consider before a transport trade is being completeint is not the only thing. The following are some other things that you should be aware of:

- ***Currency appreciation Low interest-rate***

By entering into carrying, an investor is able to make a profit from or split between a high interest-rate currency and a low interest-rate currency by entering into carrying trade. However, traffic may become unprofitable if, for some cause (like the former example of risk aversion), the low rate currency is highly valued.

Apart from rising investment risk aversion, improving economic conditions in a low-interest-paying country can also contribute to an appreciation of its currency. An ideal carrying trade requires a low-interest currency with a poor economy with low growth expectations. However, if the economy improves, the country may then give investors greater returns by growing interest rates. If this happens — as like the previous example, claims that Switzerland has raised its offered interest rates — then investors will benefit from these higher rates through investment in Swiss francs. The competitiveness of the Australian dollar – Swiss francs will be adversely impacted by the strengthening of the Swiss franc. (At least, higher interest rates in Switzerland will have a negative effect on the profitability of the carriage trade by decreasing the interest rate spread.) For example, the same sequence of events can currently take place in Japanese Yen. The Japanese yen is a perfect low-interest currency for carriage trades (known as "yen carriage trades") because of its zero interest rates. However, this situation can change. Recently, growing optimism about the Japanese economy contributed to a rise in the Japanese stock market. Increased demand for Japanese stocks and currencies induced an appreciation of the yen, and this appreciation of Yen has a negative effect on the profitability of transportation trade like the Australian dollar relative to the Japanese yen (high-interest rate).

The yen exchange will become increasingly unprofitable if investors continue to buy the yen. This further shows that the low-interest-rate currency in a transportation transaction (which is the currency to be sold) has a negative effect on the return on the transportation trade.

- ***Trade Balances***

Country trade balances can also affect the competitiveness of the transport sector (the gap between imports and exports). We have seen how capital flows from low-interest-rate payment currency to high-interest-rate payment currency when investors have higher risk-aversion. But this is not always the case.

Talk of the situation in the United States to understand why. The US is currently paying low historical interest rates, thus attracting investment from other nations, even if investors are low-risk aversion (i.e., investing in countries with high-interest rates). Why does this happen? The reason is that the US has a huge trade surplus (their imports are higher than their exports), a gap that other countries will finance. Irrespective of its interest rates, the US attracts capital flows to fund its trade deficit.

The aim of this example is to demonstrate that large trade imbalances can lead to an appreciation of low-interest rates even in cases of low-risk aversion. And if the low-interest currency in the transportation trade appreciates (the currency to be sold), it adversely affects the profitability of the transportation trade.

- ***Time Horizon***

Overall, a carry exchange is a long-term policy. Time Horizon An investor should be willing to commit to a period of at least six months before joining a carry trade. This dedication helps ensure that the "noise" of short-term currency price fluctuations will not impact trade. Furthermore, not using unnecessary leveraging for transport businesses would encourage traders to remain longer and better on the weather market by not stopping.

To sum up: Carry trading, investors should know before they trade factors like currency appreciation, trade balance, and time horizon. Any or all of these factors can make relatively profitable trading unprofitable.

ESSENTIAL TRADING STRATEGY: STAYING ON TOP OF MACROECONOMIC EVENTS

Short-term traders tend to be focused solely on the financial announcement of the week and its effect on day-to-day trading. This functions well for many traders, but it is also vital not to lose sight of the big events that can occur in the economy — or the planet. The explanation is that big macroeconomic events will drive and shift markets. Their effect goes beyond a simple shift in prices for a day or two, as such events, depending on their size and nature, can alter the fundamental perception of the currency for months or even years at a time. Things such as war, political unrest, natural disasters and major international meetings are so powerful because of the anomalies that they have significant psychological and physical effects on the currency market. Such incidents contribute to both appreciating currencies and depreciating currencies just as dramatically. Therefore, amid global developments, knowing and forecasting the fundamental course of consumer sentiment before and after such events may be highly profitable or at least help to avoid major losses.

Big Events:

- Major G-7 and G-8 meetings of finance ministers

- Presidential polls
- Significant peak
- Big meetings of central banks
- Future currency changes
- Debt defaults by major countries probable
- Potential conflicts due to rising geopolitical tensions
- Semi-annual congressional testimony of the president of the Federal Reserve

Examples are the best way to emphasize the importance of these cases.

- ***G-7 Meeting (Dubai, September 2003)***

The members of the G-7 are the United States, the United Kingdom, Japan, Canada, Italy, Germany, and France. Such countries collectively account for two-thirds of global economic output. Not all meetings of the G-7 are relevant. Just when significant changes are planned, does the market finally take place at the G7 Finance Ministers 'Meeting. The meeting of the G7 Finance Ministers on 22 September 2003 was a very critical market turning point. The dollar plummeted dramatically after the G7 finance ministers agreed to see "more flexibility in exchange rates." While these terms were somewhat bland, the market interpreted this strategy as a big move. The last time this degree was updated was in 2000.

In 2000, the market concentrated on the upcoming meeting, as the day before the meeting, there was heavy intervention in the

EUR / USD. The September 2003 meeting was also necessary because the U.S. trade deficit blew up and became a massive problem. The EUR / USD suffered the brunt of the dollar decline as Japan and China actively interfered with their currencies. In this way, the G7 Finance Ministers, in general, were generally expected to make a statement that was highly critical of Japan and China's interference policies. As shown in Figure 10.9, before the conference, the U.S. dollar had already started to sell. The EUR / USD shot up 150 pipes at the time of the launch. Although this initial change was not quite significant, the dollar decreased by eight percent in terms of trade, 9 percent compared to the British pound, 11 percent compared to the Euro, 7% against the Yen, and 1.5% compared to the Canadian dollar between September 2003 and February 2004 (the next G7 meeting). In order to take the percentages into account, an 11 percent change is equal to about 1,100 pipes. Therefore, the longer-term effect is much more important than the immediate impact, as the event itself will change the overall market feeling. Figure 10.9 is a weekly EUR / USD chart that shows how the currency pair was applied following the G-7 meeting of 22 September 2003.

- ***Political Uncertainty: 2004 United States. Presidential Elections***

The presidential elections in the US in 2004 are another example of a significant event impacting the currency market. Political uncertainty usually triggers perceived currency weakness. In addition to discrepancies in the positions of candidates on the increasing budget deficit, the highly contested presidential elections in November 2004 culminated in a complete bias in the dollar. The feeling was aggravated even more because of the government's decision to overthrow Saddam Hussein's lack of foreign support for the elected chairman (George W. Bush). As a result, the euro rose 600 pipes relative to the US dollar within three weeks of the referendum. Figure 10.10 demonstrates this. With the Bush win more and more apparent and later confirmed, the dollar sold off to the international market as the market looked forward to what would undoubtedly end up preserving the status quo. A further 200 pipes rose on the day after the election, and a further 700 pipes continued to grow before peaking six weeks later. The whole move was for two months, which may seem like years for many, but this macroeconomic occurrence really changed the markets; huge gains could have been made by those who followed it. However, this is significant even for short-term traders as since the market was generally weird dollars amounting to the United States presidential election, a more sensible trade would have looked for ways to buy EUR / USD in a bottom line rather than trying to sell rallies and lookup tops.

- ***Wars: US War in Iraq***

Geopolitical threats like conflicts may also have a pronounced impact on the currency market. Figure 10.11 shows that the dollar depreciated by 9 percent from the Swiss franc (USD / CHF) between December 2002 and February 2003 in the months leading to the invasion of Iraq. However, the amount of dollars sold off because the war itself was overwhelmingly unpopular among the world community. The Swiss-franc was actually one of the main beneficiaries due to the political neutrality and security of the country. Between February and March, the market started to believe that the war would inevitably turn into the US rapid and definitive victory. This ultimately led to a rally of USD / CHF 3 percent as investors exited their place in the short dollar.

Every occurrence has brought about large-scale currency market fluctuations, which have made important events for all forms of traders. Holding broad-based macroeconomic events aware can allow traders to make smarter decisions and prevent them from fading into the background of significant uncertainties. Most of these developments are analyzed, analyzed, and predicted by economists, currency analysts, and the international community in general several months in advance. World shifts and monetary traders must be prepared for this.

COMMODITY PRICES AS AN INDICATOR

Predictor Gold and Oil commodities have a significant relation to FX. An understanding of the relationship between them and currencies can also help traders calculate risk, change in forecast prices, and understand exposure. Although commodities look like a completely foreign idea, gold and oil appear to move mainly because of similar fundamental factors affecting monetary markets. As mentioned earlier, the Australian dollar, the Canadian dollar, the New Zealand dollar, and the Swiss franc are all four major currencies. AUD, CAD, NZD, and CHF are all strongly correlated with gold prices, natural gold reserves, and currency laws leading to almost mirror-like movements in those countries. The CAD is also somewhat in keeping with oil prices, but the relation is much more complicated and fictitious. Growing currency has a specific connection and explanation of why its behavior so well represents commodity prices. Kenntnis of the dynamics, pace, and power of these developments could be an efficient way to discover patterns in both markets.

The Relationship

Gold

First of all, it is imperative to understand the connection between gold and the U.S. dollar before examining the relation of gold to commodity currencies. Since the US is the second-largest producer of gold in the world (after South Africa), a gold price rally will not carry a dollar appreciation. When the dollar falls, gold appears to rise, and vice versa. This seemingly unlogical phenomenon is a by-product of the interpretation of gold by investors. During uncertain financial times, traders appear to be scared of the dollar and turn gold instead into a safe haven to invest. Many traders simply call gold the "anti-dollar." Thus, if this currency depreciates, gold is moved from a falling greenback to a stable commodity as cautious investors flock. The currency pairs AUD / USD, NZD / USD, and USD / CHF seem to represent the movements of gold as closest as all these other currencies have major natural and political relationships with metal.

From the South Pacific point of view, AUD / USD is very closely linked to gold (0.80), and as gold prices rise, AUD / USD also appears to increase as the Australian dollar is up against the American dollar. The explanation is that Australia is the third-largest producer of gold in the world to export about $5 billion of precious metal per year. As a result, the currency pair doubles the impact of gold rates. If volatility triggers price increases, this possibly means that the USD has already begun to depreciate. The pairing would be further downgraded as gold-demand importers more Australia's currency to meet higher costs. The New Zealand dollar continues to follow the same direction in AUD / USD pairing, despite the clear link between the New Zealand economy and Australia. In this pairing, the connection is also around 0.80 with gold. The CAD / USD association with gold prices is even greater at 0.84, mainly due to similar explanations for the link with AUD; Canada is the fifth-largest exporter of gold.

Throughout Europe, the Swiss currency is also closely linked to gold values. However, the 0.88 association between CHF / USD and metal is caused by different factors than the NZD, AUD, and CAD correlations. Switzerland has no major natural gold reserves such as Australia or Canada and is thus recognized as a metal exporter. The Swiss franc is, therefore, one of the few global currencies still compliant with the gold standard. A full 25% of the Swiss bank bills are backed up by gold reserves. This strong currency base makes no secret about why CHF in uncertain times is viewed as a safe currency haven. During moments of global instability, the Swiss appear to come together. An example of that can be seen in America's war buildup in Iraq. Most investors took their capital from the USD and aggressively invested in gold as well as CHF.

Therefore, if a trader sees a rise in gold prices (or in other metals such as copper or nickel), then either of the four commodity currencies might be prudent. The rare opportunity to convey the same dream but also to receive meaningful rewards is an important incentive to AUD / USD instead of gold. Gold is typically also a strong predictor of the overall metal market image.

Oil

Global oil prices have a significant effect both on consumers and producers in the world economy. The relationship between this commodity and currency prices is, therefore, much more complicated and less predictable. Indeed, only one (CAD) tends to be related to oil prices from all commodity currencies.

The USD / CAD has −0,4, which is a very weak number, which indicates that an increase in oil prices can only often result in the rally of the Canadian dollar. This connection was much greater during the second half of 2004 and the first half of 2005. Although Canada is the 14th largest oil producer in the world, the influence of oil on its economy is much more extensive than gold. While gold prices do not spill dramatically into other regions, oil prices certainly do. Canada has problems in particular because of its cold climate, which most of the year generates great demand for heating oil. In addition, Canada is especially vulnerable to weak international economic conditions because it is highly dependent on exports. Therefore, the impact of oil on the Canadian dollar is quite mixed. Much of this depends on how American energy demand reacts to rising oil prices. The Canadian economy is tightly tied to its southern neighbor because 85% of its exports are for the US.

Trading Opportunities

There are two ways to leverage this information now that the relationships have been clarified. In general, commodity prices are a significant predictor of currency values. This is most evident in the relationship between NZD / USD-gold and CAD / USD-oil. Commodity block traders will also track gold and oil prices to forecast currency pair movements. The second way to use this information is to use different products to express the same view, which helps to diversify risk even with a high correlation. In addition, one significant advantage is that traders can gain interest on positions based on the interest rate that is a way differential between these two countries in currencies with respect to commodity, but gold and oil future positions do not.

USING BOND SPREADS AS AN INDICATOR FOR FOREX TRADING

However, any trader can attest that interest rates are an important part of investment decision making and can lead the markets in either direction. The FOMC rate decisions are the second-largest release of unemployment data on the currency-market movement. The effects of interest rate increases have not only short-term but also long-term impacts on the currency markets. The rate decision of one central bank could affect more than one pairing in the interrelated forex market. Fixed-income-instruments such as London Interbank Offered Rates (LIBOR) and 10-year bond yields may be used as the leading currency trading indexes. For FX exchange, the interest rate differential is the difference between the base currency interest rate (first in the pair) and the quoted currency interest rate (second in a pair). Every day at 5 p.m. EST, on currency markets closing the day, funds are either paid out or collected to compensate for discrepancies in the interest rate. It can be very useful to consider the connection between interest rate differentials and currency pairs. Besides central bank decisions on overnight rates, expected future overnight rates and the expected schedule of rate changes are also important for currency pair movements. This works because most international investors are earnings seekers. Bigger investment banks, hedge funds, and institutional investors have the ability to access global markets on a capital basis. Consequently, they deliberately move funds from lower returns to higher returns.

Interest Rate Differentials: Leading Indicator, Indicator Of Chance, Or Indicator Of Labeling?

Given that most currency traders find current and future interest rate differences in the decision-making of investment, logically, there should be a link between yield differences and currency pairs. Do currency price pairs, however, predict rate decisions that make rate choices impact currency price pairs? Leading indicators are economic indicators which forecast future events; economic indicators that differ from economic events are coincident indicators; lagging indicators are economic indicators that follow an event. For example, where interest rate differentials predict future currency pair prices, interest rate differential measures of currency pair prices are said to be leading. It is dependent on how many traders worry about future rates versus current rates that interest rate differentials are a leading chance or delaying predictor of currency price pairs. Assuming that efficient markets are successful if currency traders only care about current interest rates and not future rates, a correlation is predicted. When currency traders take into account current and future interest rate differentials, they will hope to be a leading indicator of future exchange rates. The theory is that if the exchange rate rises for a certain currency, the currency usually appreciates against other currencies. In Australia, for example, where the current 10-year government bond yield is 5.50%, and the actual 10-year government bond yield is 2.00%, the yield difference will turn out to be 350-basis points in favor of Australia. In case Australia raised its interest rates by 25 basis points and the Government's 10-year bond yield by up to 5.75 percent, Australia would have a new yield spread of 375 basis points. Based on historical data, the Australian dollar in this scenario is also expected to increase compared to the US dollar. Thanks to a three-year analysis of empirical data from January 2002 to January 2005, interest rate differentials were shown to be a key indicator of currency pairs.

In a very long time, interest rate differential analysis seems more successful. However, adjustments in the outlook for the rate path over the short term can also be a leading indicator for currency prices.

Following The Currency Pair Trends and Calculating the Interest Rate Differentials

The easiest way to use interest rate differentials for trading is to keep track of a one-month LIBOR rate or 10-year bond yield in Microsoft Excel. They are calculating the interest rate difference.

Such prices are available publicly on websites like Bloomberg.com. Interest rate differentials are determined by extracting the second currency yield in the pair from the first yield. It is necessary to ensure that variations in the interest rate are measured in the order in which they appear. For example, the rate differentials in GBP / USD should be 10 years below the 10-year US average. The cost of the Treasury note. Using German 10-year bond data for euro results. Shape a table. Create a table. When ample data is collected, you can use a two-axis graph to analyze currency pairs and yields for correlations and trends. To order to use these data entirely for trading, you want to pay careful attention to patterns to currency pairs 'interest rate differentials.

FUNDAMENTAL TRADING STRATEGY: RISK REVERSALS

Risk inversions are a valuable method for applying your mix of trading indicators. One of the drawbacks of the currency exchange is the lack of volume data and precise calculation measures. The only public study on the positioning is the study of the Commodity Futures Trading Commission on 'Engagements of Traders,' and it too comes with a three-day delay. One useful alternative is to use the news plug-in Forex Capital Markets (FXCM) for real-time risk reversals under Options. Risk-reversal consists of a pair of options (a call and a put) for the same currency. On the basis of put/call parity, many more than 25 Delta options at the same expiry and strike price would also have the same implied volatility. In fact, however, this is not valid. The sentence is rooted in uncertainty, which allows a good instrument for evaluating market feelings. A number of calls strongly in support of places suggest that there is more demand for calls than places. The reverse is also true: a big number in favor of call-over suggests that the higher demand means that a premium is built-in options. If risk reversals are close to zero, this means that the bulls and bears have indecision and that there is no clear market bias.

How Does Risk Reversal Table Look like?

Each abbreviation of the currency options is listed, and, as indicated, most risk reversals are close to zero, suggesting no major prejudice. However, for USD / JPY, longer-term reversals suggest that yen calls (JC) and dollar puts are strongly preferred on the market.

How to Use the Information

The positive and negative integer may be used for simpler printing and tracking purposes for calling and pricing. Therefore, a positive number means that calls are preferred to calls and that the whole market expects the underlying currency to push upwards. Similarly, a negative number means that puts are favored over calls and that the market expects the underlying currency to be downwards. Danger reversals can be used prudently as a valuable tool to determine market positioning. Although the signals produced by a risk inversion system are not fully accurate, they may indicate when the market is bullish or bearish. Danger reversals are very significant when the values are extreme. Extreme rates are defined as one standard difference plus or minus the average risk reverse. If risk revolutions are on these rates, they send contrary signals that a currency pair is overbooked or overbooked on the basis of feelings. The indicator is seen as a contrary warning because it makes it much harder for the currency to surge when the whole market is primed for an increase in a given currency and thus much more likely for it to drop down on adverse news or events. As a consequence, a strongly negative statistic implies over-volumes, while a strongly positive number implies voluminous. While risk reversals are not ideal for buying or selling signals, they may provide additional information to make trading decisions.

USING VOLATILITIES TO TRACK MARKET MOVEMENTS

Since this is a very useful approach that is a favorite among experienced hedge funds, it definitely deserves a more detailed explanation. The implied volatility can be defined as a measure of the expected currency fluctuation over a given period based on fluctuations in previous prices. Usually, this is determined by taking the average annual price variance. Potential values contribute to the calculation of implied uncertainty used to measure optional premiums. While it sounds very complex, it does not apply. Basically, option volatility calculates, based on historical fluctuations, the rate, and magnitude of a currency's price over some time. If thus the average daily trading range of EUR / USD contracts ranged from 100 pipes to 60 pipes and remained there for two weeks, short-term volatility was also likely significantly contracted compared with long-term volatility over the same duration.

Guidelines

So, there are two basic rules to follow as a guideline. First, if short-term option volatility is considerably lower than long-term volatility, one should predict a split, although that rule does not specify the path of the breakdown. Second, if short-term volatility options are substantially higher than long-term volatility, a reversal to the trading range can be expected.

Why Do These Guidelines Work?

In the ranging period, the volatility of the implied option is either small or rising. The reason for these laws is that there appears to be little change in times of range trading. We worry about the sharp decline in volatility options, which may be a sign of a lucrative breakdown. If short-term volatility is higher than long-term volatility, short-term market behavior is more volatile than the long-term average price index. This implies that the ranges will gradually return to average levels. The pattern in empirical evidence is most evident. Here are some examples of how this rule forecasts patterns or breaks accurately.

It is important to note before we evaluate the charts that we use one-month volatility as our short-term volatility and three-month volatility as our long-term volatility.

Benefiting From the Guidelines

This technique is not only useful for traders with breakouts but can also be used by range traders to forecast a possible breakup scenario. If volatility contracts drop significantly or become very small, the likelihood of continuing retail trade decreases. After looking at a historical range, traders will look at volatility in order to estimate the probability that the place will stay within this range. If the trader wants to stay for a long time or short, he or she should keep track of volatility so long as he or she has an open position in the pair to help them decide when to close this role. If short-term volatility falls well below long-term volatility, the trader will consider closing the position unless the suspected outbreak is preferred by the trader. The future break will probably work for the trader if the current location is near the limit and far from the stop. In this theory, it can be helpful to exclude restricted prices from current spot prices to maximize benefits from the future split. When the spot price is near the stop price, and far away from the limit price, it is possible that the break works against the trader.

Breakdown traders can track volatility to detect a breakdown. If a trader suspects a breakdown, this breakdown can be confirmed by implied volatility. If implied volatility is constant or increased, the currency is more likely to continue trading in range than if the volatility is small or decreasing. In other words, breakout traders will aim for short-term volatility before they start trading substantially less than long-term volatility.

In addition to being a key price factor, option volatility can also be a valuable tool for forecasting market behavior. Optional volatility measures the rate and extent of currency price fluctuations. Implied option volatility measures, on the other hand, based upon historical fluctuations, the predicted variations in the price of a currency over a certain period of time.

Monitoring Volatility on Your Own

The analysis of volatility on your own volatility typically includes the traditional annual variance from regular price adjustments. The FXCM news plug-in available at www.fxcm.com/forex-data-softwareexchange.jsp will provide volatility. In general, we use three-month volatilities for long-term volatilities and one-month for short-term volatilities. The next step is to start building a list of dates, currency price pairs implied one-month volatility and implied three-month volatility of currency pairs. The easiest way to produce this list is to create a tablet software like Microsoft Excel, which enables the graphics of trends. The difference between one month and three months of volatility may also be helpful when looking for significant variations or measuring volatility for one month as the percentage of three months of volatility.

When enough data is collected, the data can be graphically represented via visual aid. The diagram will use two y-axes, one with spot trading and the other with short and long-term volatility. If required, the short-term and long-term volatile differences can also be charted in a single y-axis graph.

CHAPTER 5 : SELECTING STOCKS FOR SWING TRADING

Investors and traders face problems when determining which stocks or indices to swing trade. And how do you settle on stocks over stocks? You need to classify the selection attributes with thousands of stocks to pick for you. A set must be finite, and the actual number of inventories depends on many variables, including:

1. ***Money available for trading***

Each plan would be constrained by the resources available for trade. You should differentiate your trading capital from a long-term portfolio. Many investors are moving a small proportion of the capital available for short-term trading away, while the rest have to reinvest in long-term investment, mutual funds, properties, and the monetary market.

2. ***The level of risk tolerance in turn***

Your specific risk tolerance level also restricts and determines the types of stocks that you use for swing trading. Companies with decades of experience, billions of money, and hegemony are relatively safe investments — not ideal for swing trading yet. Relatively young companies tend to produce the price volatility ideal for swing trading. Nonetheless, they can be overly dangerous. Many people would describe their risk tolerance so that their stock options fall between these extremes.

3. *Price swing degree and current trend*

Swing trading operates in a price instability middle zone. If the trading range of a stock is small and not at all flexible, there will be limited trading opportunities. If there is a stock on the other end of the spectrum, with wildly fluctuating prices and no established trade range, you have another problem: price may not follow the normal "rules" of swing trade, candlestick charts, and other technical methods for forecasting price movement. Highly volatile resources do not always obey, so there is actually no predictability.

4. *Preferences for personal use*

All have their favorite stocks. You may decide to swing trading in inventories you own or stocks that you have monitored over time. However, you may as well decide to specialize in a limited number of industries and switch from one industry to another based on cyclical trends. In pursuing personal preferences, it is important to recognize limiting factors rather than technological signals. You can tend to ignore important signals because you prefer stock or because your preferences are small; you ignore a broad range of stocks.

5. *Technical and simple tests*

You choose either simple or advanced measures to (1) pick or (2) delete the inventory from the list of candidates in swing trading.

It is a mistake to use just one selection criterion; you should mix several fundamental and technical criteria, minimize the list of risk rates and stocks, and align market patterns with clear basic principles.

Thumb Rules for Stock Selection

It makes sense to start picking stocks for swing trading by identifying a variety of possible businesses that meet fundamental criteria. Even traders focused solely on technical price, and volume metrics must accept the fundamentals as a measure for (1) stock price risk, (2) capital strength or weakness, and (3) long-term price growth potential. The fundamentals are retroactive in the sense that current financial reporting is historical, but underlying developments and capital strength measures still demonstrate future opportunities at the technological level.

Once you include them in a list of swing trade possibilities, you should ask some very important questions about businesses, such as things outside sales and earnings or the current capitalization. Ask these questions as a way to narrow your swing trade list:

1. ***Has the company ever posted a net profit?***

A listed company will disclose profitable operations at a minimum requirement. Many businesses have years of failure, and this may be part of a normal business period. Many companies have never made a profit. That means that the current value is dependent on future growth expectations, and there can be a lot of difficulty in the price equation. The years dot.com make this lesson good; a company should have posted any profits in the last years before it should be taken seriously for swing trading.

2. *Has management been scandalous?*

Recent history has shown that many famous businesses can be poorly managed. There is no point in investing in the stock of a company with questionable accounts or whose administration is investigated. These issues manipulate markets and can disrupt normal cyclical patterns, preventing time, and predicting how short-term prices will be.

3. *Were the profits reasonably stable or irregular?*

Consistency is a reliable measure of a company's reliability. Have wages and taxes been stable and regular? What are the annual reports sporadic and incoherent? Price volatility is highly emphasized, but fundamental volatility is also an examination. Erratic reported income is a sign of mismanagement, dubious change in accounting, or chaos in the business. Any of these could also impact the reliability of price trends. Test core revenues to assess the accuracy of the reporting of a client. Such earnings are published as part of the S&P inventory survey, measured by Standard & Poor's, provided for free by certain discount brokerage platforms, such as Charles Schwab & Company (http:/www.schwab.com). The accuracy of core income is as critical as a fully recorded benefit.

4. Is the company a market leader?

Then, does it offer a product that is not outdated? The concurrence also determines profitability. A business leading the industry, therefore, has a range of attributes in stock prices. If the prices of the market leader rise or decrease, the remaining rivals in the same sector continue to do so. A business does not need to be number one in the industry to justify Swing Trading, but, like many other businesses, the leader also sets the tone of trading.

Over time, there is obsolescence in certain items. That is unavoidable. And, if a company can not change over time, its whole product line will be threatened. For example, Polaroid filed bankruptcy a few years ago. The photo industry created a revolution but did not keep up with new digital technology. In recent years, Kodak, historically dominant in the film distribution market, has also fallen behind as multiple rivals have passed the company in the creation of digital technology — so that Kodak relied to some degree on its film lines, so he could not see how much the whole business changed. Such forms of emerging technological developments provide an insight into how businesses grow over time or, in some cases, are behind their more aggressive rivals. This impacts both long-term interest and short-term price trends. While swing trading is a short-term business strategy, restricting this behavior to profitable and well-managed companies that are most likely to have short term "typical" or "normal" stock price behavior.

5. ***Is the company diversified? Is it immune to cyclical problems?***

Many ways of diversification exist. Most people think that capital is the most evident type of diversification in many different goods. However, this may also mean investing in new markets or products, avoiding inventories vulnerable to the same cycles, or allocating capital to entirely different markets. Diversification within the organization itself applies to specific product or service lines of business. Altria Corporation (MO) is, for example, best known for its company Phillip Morris, but it has Kraft Foods, which diversifies its overall assets into a completely different market. Taking about the manner in which you accumulate stocks, the topic of internal diversification is as relevant as most investors understand portfolio-related types.

A not well-diversified business is prone to cyclical shifts. One way to offset this cyclical issue is through diversification into lines other than the main retail line, for example, when consumer buying patterns are in a down cycle.

6. *What are the current problems facing the company?*

Everything else do you need to know when you select businesses except for the latest and historical financial reports? Was there an unresolved legal problem or future trade union disputes? Companies that rely on large unionized workers, for example, are vulnerable to strikes. And lengthy trials also have a negative impact on productivity. As of 2006, Merck (MRK) had thousands of pending cases because of the widely documented Vioxx product ill effects. And over many years, the tobacco industry has faced thousands of lawsuits. Such problems can adversely affect the value of a company or, if the company prevails or falls less than expected, stock prices might also increase. There is also no excuse by itself to avoid a corporation or industry through the presence of thousands of lawsuits. It is, however, one of the extra-financial considerations, in addition to litigation, any other form of contingent liability that affects a company's value and its expected value and should be checked as part of your decision for purchase or not.

7. *Was the organization big enough to have a track record?*

It is difficult to make a sound decision without a track record when choosing one stock over another. How long did the business last? Can you say whether net value growth or a decrease has occurred? What is management's reputation? Is the company paying dividends, and what is the total dividend return? Was the payment of the dividend accurate, or was any missed? These questions describe companies and give you a way to compare and choose.

Technical and Fundamental Indicators

A combination of basic and technical indicators will help to narrow the list of swing trading stocks. If your selection criteria are too broad, too many stocks will be available to choose from. Ideally, a group of 10 to 25 stocks meeting all your requirements is a fair range, especially when they represent a diverse cross-section of the markets. If you can test the basic strength of a stock by using only four or five indicators, it is a sound number. Too many metrics will make it difficult to pick stocks, not least because the tests have to be run and tracked too long. The key indicators suggested include:

1. *Revenue and profits*

Revenue and profits or the top and bottom lines of the financial statement are a sound and important starting point. This is a financial statement that reports all operations for a certain duration (year, quarter, or month). If you track your income and earnings over time, you will assess whether a business is constantly growing; reports incorrect results, or lines its performance. For example, Lucent Technologies' (LU) sales and income for the five years 2001 to 2005 were inconsistent, as shown in Figure 6.1. Notice that both sales and earnings have changed significantly from year to year.

Lucent's five years have been quite unpredictable not only because of dramatic cuts in recorded sales but also because of significant changes in net losses and profits. In contrast, Wal-Mart (WMT) posted remarkably consistent sales and earnings.

2. *Return on dividend*

The net income from which you receive the purchase of stocks is not limited to the benefit of the purchase and selling of shares. If you hold stock for any length of time, you must also compare the stock dividend yield. This type of profit, also known as a current return, can represent a significant part of the overall income.

3. *Ratio P / E*

The value for money or the P / E ratio is a common measure of the current price of a product. It contrasts a technical factor (actual stock price) with a fundamental factor (earnings per share). The multiple (the product of price division by profit) reflects the expectation of the consumer for future growth. In other words, the higher the number, the longer the risk. One method of selecting stocks is to restrict the P / E size. For example, you may decide to limit your stocks to those with multiples ranging from 11 to 25.

4. *The amount of debt*

One of the most important corporate health tests is an analysis of the pattern in capitalization. A business may finance its activities through equity (selling stocks) or debt capital (issuing bonds or obtaining long-term loans). The higher the amount of the debt, the higher the burden on potential cash. All debt capital must be paid back by interest. If debt capital is too high, potential growth will be impeded, and there will be fewer dividends as more revenues are paid in interest. So the debt ratio is one of the main checks you should carry out. To measure, divide the long-term liabilities balance by the total capitalization (long-term debt plus equity), which reflects the result as a percentage. This is a negative sign when this amount increases over time.

Limiting the basics is crucial because you cannot make important distinctions between companies with too much knowledge. Some solid, significant tests covering rentability and capital strength are necessary for the selection of stocks. The same is true of technological measures. In this field, however, your target is quite different. You are looking for signs of success and a stable income with the basics. You want stocks from the technical side that is not highly volatile but also not flat. The range of useful technical indicators includes:

1. *Trading range*

The trading range is the most basic price predictor. A very limited range of trade, with low volatility, defines stock as low risk, and a wide range of trade, implying high volatility, defines stock as a high risk. An inventory so unpredictable that there can be no fixed trading range is extremely risky. You want to find stocks with mild volatility for swing trading. If volatility is equated with market value, you can understand why moderate volatility is important. When both buyers and sellers are involved in the stock, there is a never-ending battle to control the price over the two to five days. Buyers want the price to rise after purchasing, and sellers just want the price to go down after sale. It is also important to recognize that buyers become sellers, vice versa if the price movement is acceptable to the interests of an investor. If the volatility is too low, this implies a limited amount of interest in inventory; and if the volatility is too high, the course of the short-term price cycles is more difficult to decide.

2. *Channel path*

The parallel movement of the trading range is a price source. If you open swing businesses with long positions, you are most interested in stocks with upstream networks. If the channel is flat, but transactions can be made within this exchange range, it doesn't matter whether you open positions on the long or short sides; you can either start or use both, depending on the formation and setup patterns.

3. *Recent history of swing rates for the short term*

The historical instability provides no future price path guarantees. But it gives you some insight into how price movements and adjustments — the pacing of moves up and down, the degree of change, and the impact of changes in the daily volume together with dramatic price shifts. 4. Latest trends, including demand gaps and breakouts.

4. Breakouts and price gaps

Technical trends are interesting not only because they provide indications for buying or selling but also because they allow you to anticipate the next step with some confidence. Breakdowns and price differences are among the most relevant technical measures because they frequently arise at the beginning of a new cycle. Even a small price gap can signify a big turning point and price breakdowns above or below support are always important. The higher the pattern of break-out, the stronger the trend. In conjunction with one or more price differences, the breakout reflects a very significant short-term price transition. This can be the most profitable swing exchange.

Short-Term and Long-Term Measures

All traders must differentiate themselves. It results from the synchronization with short-term swing trade structure indications of long-term fundamental and technical indicators. The conditions are both so unique that they cannot be ignored. You first determine which stocks will be included in the field of swing trading. Some of these stocks may be purchased and retained by you. This long-term optimism must be constrained because most people can not afford thousands or hundreds of inventories. In order to establish the requirements as a point of departure, you must purchase a few shares.

Thousands of stocks, indices, and money traded share the swing network signals. It doesn't mean you want to do business randomly and disciplinarily. One of the problems is how to limit their range of operations for swing traders. Through first deciding how to collect stocks, you can achieve the necessary limitations. Five criteria to be considered:

1. ***Apply basic technical and moral principles***

In this chapter, a few primary indicators have previously been introduced to demonstrate how the range of tests in picking stocks can be reduced for both long term and swing trading. You will note that the conditions for both are the same. When you expect to swing the trade and do not keep inventories in your portfolio, even if you prepare for a typical two- to five-day cycle to switch to and from positions, your risk profile should always be checked by how inventories are stockpiled. The criteria limit the number of stocks you use for swing trading. When you end up with around 15-20 shares, you will be able to keep track of swing trading opportunities on a regular basis, and all of these suit your analytical requirements. It is doubtful that you will never face a situation in which there are no swing market conditions.

2. ***Enable useful asset sector decisions***

Investor classes are favored by a single investor. You might be scared of investing, for example, in grocery, oil, and gas, or computer industries. These assumptions can be based either on past experience or a greater than average sense of risk. Some sectors are naturally more competitive in some economic times than others. If the priorities are moral or not, it is necessary to avoid sectors:

- You're uncomfortable for you.
- You assume that there is a high risk.
- You don't get what's perfect.

3. ***Concentrate on-field leaders***

Within a specific market, it makes sense to shift trade within topics that are considered to be leaders. The explanation is sound: non-leading stocks in one sector seem to follow the general guidelines of the leading stocks. It is useful to concentrate on these managers for swing trading purposes for basic setup signals. Most swing traders depend on metrics and funds in the market, but this is less successful. When you buy an ETF in a market, for example, you invest in a mixture of strong and weak stocks, and the net result is compensatory. Single stock trading is easier to make the most of swing trading.

3. ***Distinguish between swing betting and swing exchange***

Pure function, therefore, is always a coin flip. Also, speculators with different types of research appear to prefer unrecovered prospects for smaller, emerging issues. Most of these organizations have never made any profit and still do not have a website. They may also lack a clear trading history. Therefore, essential measures such as volatility, "typical" daily volumes, and institutional holdings can not be measured or reviewed. Swing is completely different. Swing is different. The price trend is easier to identify among well-established shares with an easily observable trading range, including retail and institutional investors. This does not mean that speculative market trading should not be swinging. It simply implies more theoretical risk, however, and it is an important distinction.

4. *Using compatible modes of trading*

Most investors trust in the long-standing traditional position. The case series is shopping. Yet short-selling is equally relevant – with the sell-hold-buy sequence. Moreover, as sales are set up, half of all short selling opportunities take place at the end of the two to five-day cycle. Therefore, one alternative is to only take long-term positions, and the other is to follow strategies that also allow you to trade by opening positions when stocks are expected to fall at prices. However, there are two (2) ways of doing this:

a. *Short selling*

Furthermore, the short-selling of stocks are significantly higher than the purchasing of stocks. Short sales are explained in the next chapter.

b. *Options*

Another way is to put options. If you sell, you benefit from lowering the stock price. Options will provide a lucrative alternative to the purchase and sale of stocks and greatly increase your potential profits from swing trading. Chapters 8 and 9 explain how options can be included in your swing trading strategy.

Price Stability and 'great' Swing Trade Stock

When you are looking for the right stock of swing trading, you have to face two opposing goals. You need the flexibility to create the structures that you have to manage in and out of stocks for these short-term changes; in other words, you have to be able to trade and know other traders 'affections. You will need to have great business value. At the same time, you don't want to take more risky stock positions than you want.

The "healthy" trading inventory should contain volatility suitable for such shorter variations in markets, but without high volatility, with high risks.

The concept of the "right" stock should be based on a study of price volatility and trade range for each individual who is entering into a swinging trading strategy. For some, the five-point range of volatility for Coca-Cola would be inadequate. For others, the 18-point General Motors exchange range of 97 percent variance would be too small. An inventory of many stocks contributes to "medium-range" inventories of volatility. It means an average of 20 to 40% variance in some meanings over a 12-month period. This supposed medium-range instability is probable given the extreme examples of General Motors and Coca-Cola. There are volatility levels throughout the place. A search of four inventories covering General Motors and Coca-Cola showed the following trade ranges and rates of volatility:

The volatility and the price range differ. An 8-point range for Citigroup at the price level of the 40s generates a 19% outcome, but at the same split point, 9 points for Pfizer at the 20s, is a 45% uncertainty. This makes an important difference between trade and uncertainty. The real volatility cannot and must not be limited to the percentage measured for the price spread over 12 months. You must also take into account the point value in the exchange range. The 18-point trading range of General Motors was quite high as opposed to the five-point range of Coca-Cola, for example. This would be true, regardless of the level of uncertainty.

This statement works by raising the volatility of stocks. For example, Altria traded between 62 and 80 but recorded only 29 percent volatility. But the price range, like General Motors, was 18 points. By contrast, the 9-point range of Pfizer posted a volatility rate of 45 percent. The basis price levels of each stock are responsible for these inequalities. Comparing price volatility between stocks may be useful in some respects but can also be misleading in the formula for establishing volatility percentages. The comparison of volatility among stocks in terms of the real trading range and the extremes of price channels makes more sense.

The following chapter analyzes short sales within a shifting trading strategy. Two chapters are accompanied by how you can use options to extend the approach and make the software more flexible.

SELLING SHORT

Going into Swing Trading With Short Order

Swing trading can be entered with one of the two-timing beliefs: (1) the price is about to increase or (2) the price is about to decrease. If you think the price will go up, you have to buy a stock for a long time. If your plan is right, the price will increase, and you can close the place to profit. When you assume that the price will fall, you need to be brief, i.e., open the transaction by ordering.

The long position includes two well-known sides in the sequence of transaction possibilities. The first side of the transaction is long when the order is described as a buy to open. And this place ends with a close-order offset offer.

The instructions occur on the short side in the opposite series. The first transaction is therefore called sell for opening, which simply means shortening the defense. This is closed with an alternative purchase.

This is a daunting idea for many people who are unfamiliar with the idea of splitting. Often the question arises, "How can I sell anything that I do not own? "The reason is that it obliges you to take one of several future actions when you go low. These include:

- Closing the position with a purchase in order to cancel a short
- Approving an exercise from a customer on the other side, if options are available.

Reverse Sequence

Imagine going to the real estate market and finding a house for sale, finding a buyer and entering into a contract, selling the house to the buyer, and only then purchasing the house from the present owners. (The next chapter includes more.)

Such behavior is hard to understand and could potentially be illegal. In this case, you have no legal right to sell or accept money because you don't own the land. But you can do just that in the stock market, and as a swing trader, one-half of your future trades will be on the short-sighted side.

This is happening because of the ups and downs of a stock and the uncertainty and covetousness of other investors. If you only use the buy setup, you can benefit from only one-half of your possibilities. So shortening is as critical as long trading. In the next chapter, you will see why stock shortening might not be necessary; however, in order to make this option for yourself, you must first analyze the operation of short sales, assess the risk involved, and whether short sales are sufficient for you.

This is how the process works. To sell a stock, you must first borrow the stock. So if you want to cut 100 shares, the brokerage company will buy these shares for you. The borrowed shares are sold on the market. If the swinging trade is timed, the value of the stock will fall, and the place can be closed for a profit. If your timetable is off and the stock price rises, you either have to sell for a loss or wait for the price trend to take place. This may lead to problems if your interpretation of the chart is incorrect, and sometimes this is certain.

Many traders will accept the risk of short selling, knowing that it is possible to avoid losses most of the time using validation measures or reduce them by curbing action. It makes sense to reduce the losses when swing trading is planned to complete the opening and closing transaction within five days or less.

The other procedural component of short sales is to borrow the stock to sell it. This implies an expense. Your investment company charges interest based on the value of the stock it borrows, the holding period, and its present rate. You are expected to deposit at least 50 percent of the stock value based on the minimum rule in place for margin borrowing. If the value increases, the brokerage firm will require extra deposit amounts to meet this margin requirement. The outstanding stock remains subject to interest and tax payments until the short position is filled, i.e., shares are bought to close the account.

Besides the margin requirement, short sales are also somewhat limited by federal rules. As part of the Stock Exchange Act of 1934, the uptick rule was introduced and recognized as law 10a-1. This says you can only sell stock on an uptick or a zero plus tick. In other terms, only if the last traded price is higher than the preceding price will you perform a short selling. The main objective of this rule was to avoid a reduction in stock price pressures by selling short, which would produce larger profits with higher short-selling rates. So when you reach a short order, you know that the order is only filled out if and when a boost happens on the stock.

Short Selling Risks

Short selling, also referred to as shortening, is designed to make money if your timing is right and the price of the stock falls. Many people are more aware of the idea of long-term or stock purchase in the expectation that its market value rises. The trade is much more complicated and entails far greater risks than long positions, while short selling can be just as lucrative as buying stock shares.

With these risks in mind, some swing traders prefer to avoid short sales and concentrate only on the quest for buying configuration. This strategy is more conservative than using both long and short opening positions. In each case, the margin rule states that the brokerage firm will deposit at least 50% of the stock value. Nonetheless, risk on the short side is potentially limitless (the inventory may rise indefinitely), while risk on the long side is minimal. The overall loss would be covered by the amount of money invested in the market value of the stock were to drop to null. However, a more pragmatic view will further reduce the future long-side danger to tangible book value.

For instance, a stock today sells at $55 per share. Short sales have unknown consequences, as stock prices per share could rise indefinitely. The estimated long-term risk for each share is $55; however, the practical average risk of the tangible book value is $20 is $35.

Risk comparisons for swing trading are difficult to make. For theory, at least, the rising and downward patterns of the swing trading market are similar. So long as the set-up intensity is the same on either side, it doesn't matter if the stock price is a response to fear or greed; the timing technique remains the same. Once you begin working, the danger picture changes drastically – whether long or short in the stock. Short sales entail much greater risk than the purchasing of shares. In view of the disparity in risk rates, short sales are not correctly perceived as "equal" to a long position as part of a shifting trading strategy. Short sales are often used by investors as part of a broader plan or hedge, one of many strategies where risks are offset in another position. For example, if you own stock and the price rises considerably, you can sell stock shortly to take advantage of a short-term correction, but you do not have to sell shares long.

Short stock sales often reward the positions of options traders and are used by hedge funds for numerous reasons.

The risk must also be perceived by swing traders in terms of dividend income on each side of the strategy. A short seller never gets a dividend, but it is a potentially significant part of the overall income. In contrast, you earn dividends when you are in a long position as long as you own the stock on or before the date of the ex-dividend. One adjustment in swing trading that entail the trading of shares with this date in mind as the value of stocks is changed after dividends are taken into account. However, for short-selling risks, there may be a significant drawback that short-sellers do not collect or gain dividends.

Likewise, the market risk for short sellers is not restricted to the swing trade. Even when you deal with deployment signals on maps, outside forces frequently distort stock prices. For example, when a large number of short-sellers simultaneously cover their positions and buy shares, this can create artificial demand, increase share prices, and nullify swinging trade timing.

The sudden reporting of a number of short positions could be triggered by normal market supply and demand processes for those shares, or institutional investors, especially hedge funds, can be actively involved. For example, the management of the fund can monitor the number of short-term transactions in a particular stock — and can note a rise in short-term positions on a particular stock, and in turn purchases other shares. This boosts short-sellers 'share price and panic, resulting in high publicity. The hedge fund then profits from the higher stock price. It represents a change in the market risk for short-run swing traders. One market theory, known as the "short-interest hypothesis," is based on the belief that rapid growth in short-term interests predicts price growth.

A distinction with respect to short sales risks is worth remembering. Many short vendors simply gamble and seek to benefit from a general stock price fall. In contrast, swing traders would be short only if a suitable setup existed. Although they have different attributes and decision-making processes, they are subject to the same market forces. The acts between short-run speculators can negatively affect swing dealers, even if they respond to the clearest of settings.

Short Selling Variants

It is easier to trade on the short side if you have shares of a portfolio. Swing trading is normally associated with fast in-and-out positions, but there is some swinging amongst investors that also have shares.

Often there are sound reasons. For instance, if you own stock shares, which you would like to keep for the long term, you can swing trade to compensate for temporary downward declines in prices and take up profits without selling shares. Swing is actually an effective and suitable strategy if you want to make profits but don't want to sell the stock.

In this scenario, you can sell the box shortly. If you own the shares already, in order to sell short, you don't have to borrow them. The term is derived in the past from the issuance and holding of share certificates in the safe deposit box. The anti-box strategy enables you to shorten your shares with no (1) loans, and interest payments to your brokerage, and (2) sell shares that you would rather hold in your portfolio.

One problem with any form of short selling is that it easily calls for stock price manipulation. The earlier example, when large investors buy shares on the basis of short-term interest increases, may lead to price rises as short-range sellers panic and cover their positions. Most investors know the pump and dump — tech to artificially inflate stock prices after the purchasing of stocks so as to increase prices — when speculators take long positions. The short-term compensatory tactic, also known as the short-term and manipulation, includes taking action to shorten certain investors with the intention of reducing the stock price. Everyone who falls short should be aware of the potential of dishonest traders to try to manipulate prices.

The SEC and NASD have both proposed rules for eliminating stock price manipulation by loading and dumping and for short-term and distorting activities. But with the widely available online investment chat lines, it is difficult to capture all abuses. Swing traders are wise to respond to chart signals and disregard rumors on the Internet.

The following two chapters propose an alternative to short sales, including options for short and long shares. With options, limited capital can be used to extend your swing trading portfolio considerably, but with substantially less risk. While options are not ideal for all, their wise but restricted use entails less risk than both long and short stocks and can yield the same level of profit.

Assessing Risks and Opportunities

Swing trading makes sense in the modern world of fast-moving trading, easy access to data and charting software, and low-cost transaction fees. However, it would not have been realistic in the past. Today, many traders realize that an investment strategy must not be structured by a stockbroker, trading costs, or research difficulties. For example, for any listed company, you will find an annual or quarterly report at this time. You don't have to order a copy from your stockbroker and wait two weeks until the mail arrives. This ultra-comfort simplifies the expansion of your investment opportunities more than ever; it also increases the risks associated with any approach. It is, therefore as necessary as ever to assess risk as part of your strategy exploration. This involves swing trade and, of course, the strategies and the risks you employ. Some facets of the rigorous risk assessment of swing trading include:

1. *The overall plan*

How much should you do with swing trading? How much capital would you put at risk and, at the same time, belong or short for each stock? Even investors who subscribe to the buy and hold strategy know that they have to diversify, and the issue of swing trading should also be posed. Even the true believer in swing trade should learn to diversify a portfolio through policy so that some money can be included in long-term securities, mutual funds, or non-stock investments.

2. *Short-term costs and risks in the long-term place*

The transaction costs of any policy are always a matter, and both the acquisition and the selling are expensive. This expense must be taken into account in the plan. The use of options is much cheaper than the purchase and sale of stocks, and multiple options contracts are very low compared with stock trading. Based on your profitable trade rate, you should be mindful of the transaction cost in your overall assessment.

3. *Short stock sale*

Most people agree that short sales are a high-risk market approach. Many investors that are not prepared to take the risk must restrict their swing trade to purchasing only so that half of all opportunities are missed. Some people can accept this risk, particularly if they have a lot of faith in recognition of their setup pattern. However, this risk can not be overlooked.

4. *Option risks*

The demand for options is risky for several reasons. Terminology is strange and complex; time is a challenge, and the difficulty of the evaluation of options will trick you. If you stress trade in short-term, low, or no-time options, you can minimize the risk. If you buy shortages instead of stocks, you eliminate the risk of short sales. However, "chance of experience" is also a choice factor. You must fully understand the market before you actually do business.

5. *Risks of diversification*

Both investors and traders must consider the many types of diversification and recognize the degree to which they are needed in their portfolio. In stocks used for swing trading, for example, you can diversify the use of several different sectors on the market and even in combinations of buy-installation and sale. Be conscious, however, of the diversification opportunities between swing trading and other strategies such as long-term purchasing and holding, option betting, covered call writing on long stocks in your portfolio, and the use of traded funds.

The distinction between chance and risk cannot be made separately. It's a common error. Many people like to concentrate on the profit potential of a particular strategy but also forget to take into account the associated risk directly. Both cannot be regarded as various aspects of an investment decision; they are two facets of the same characteristics. The potential for benefit and risk for any plan are inseparable. This is something worth remembering because only the good side of things can be focused on.

Danger can also be seen as a way to test yourself. Many tactics seem to be both thrilling and successful on paper. You can quickly convince yourself that you have a "safe thing." In swing trading, you can observe the continuity of past price behavior on a narrow range or enclosing track. That's not the case, though. They work most of the time, but stock prices can still ignore the signals and shift in the 'right' direction. This is characterized as a path that produces a loss rather than a benefit, which always needs to be taken into account.

Risk Profile Diversification

One of the most important varieties of diversification is focused on your personal risk profile. Any risk discussion is based on the general assumption that everyone has a particular, specific level of risks and that all investments in the portfolio must comply with that profile. This is never true in practice. Many individuals are more nuanced and cannot be so narrowly defined.

For instance, you may adopt a very conservative attitude towards home and saving costs in your family, but a higher risk position for your stock portfolio. Your home is secured and maintained, and you might even avoid an unnecessary hypothetical temptation, realizing the amount of cash and equity versus the level of debt. Your savings account can yield relatively low rates, but it is insured. These are very conservative investment types.

Your inventory portfolio may be somewhat more violent. You may be willing to take some risk in the hope of overcoming market averages. You can buy certain long-term stocks, bring those funds into mutual funds, and use the remainder of your funds in stock options or speculation. This is where swing trading is involved; you can split the overall portfolio into many different segments and identify different rates of risks. Your investments in the "safety net" (home and saving) should be very cautious, your stock portfolio could be somewhat volatile, and some of your shares may be swing trading by taking short positions or long options.

When you identify each segment and monitor the rates of funds invested in each segment, you can diversify not only according to investment styles (real estate, money market, and equity) but also according to the risk profile. This approach, known as asset allocation, is not always described in terms of personal risk. It is discussed more often in terms of market diversification. It is also possible to diversify between markets while staying in line with a narrowly defined level of risk. The above example shows how the allocation of assets can also be used to improve your own diversification of risk.

The distribution of assets is most frequently described in percentages. While each investor is different, some market analysts have tried, based on current economic conditions, to assign a standardized percentage recommendation. In this variation, each investor will respond to the changing economic conditions in the same way. Nonetheless, it makes more sense to interpret the distribution of assets as a risk-based change in a portfolio. For example, it might not be useful to spend all your investment assets on swing trading. For example, you can diversify your college, retirement, and income portfolio. The overall goals of each segment in your portfolio determine the correct risk levels; in that regard, swing trading may be acceptable, but it should be focused on the conservatism of the investment goal itself.

In all cases, no one can be accurately described as a "conservative" investor or a "speculator." Several variables, including:

1. ***Understanding of Particular Market***

It can help to determine the goods and risks you choose, your awareness of a particular market.

If you understand a business completely, you are more likely to participate. Some markets fear people because they are complex; options, for example, are not as dangerous as many people perceive. However, the meanings and unique features of options make it especially confusing for anyone who doesn't know how they function. The more you understand how a market works, the better you can decide how you can use the goods.

2. *Preferred risk rates and capacity to jeopardize funds*

Individuals tend to invest money in particular ways. Some of them are extremely cautious and will generally accept lower than average returns in order to avoid risk. Others are more likely to gamble in exchange for far greater risks, hoping for exceptionally high returns. Many people are between these extremes somewhere.

3. *Present rates of income and assets*

Your risk profile changes as your revenue increases, and your net value increases or decreases. A new career or work, divorce, or other major economic changes in your life will also impact your risk profile directly. It is important that you are aware of these changes and that you can change your portfolio to suit your current situation.

4. *Degree of fear of the economic future*

As economic and political attitudes change, the risk profile will change. Even if you don't suffer from fluctuations in interest rates or oil prices, the entire market responds to these matters, and that also affects your performance on a particular market or strategy.

CHAPTER 6 : DAY TRADING AND SWING TRADING - THE DIFFERENCE

Active traders also form two camps: day traders and swing traders. Both tend to benefit from short-term stock fluctuations (versus long-term investments), but which is the better trading strategy? Here are the advantages and disadvantages of day trading and swing trade.

Day trading requires a very special set of skills that is difficult to learn. Becoming a Day Trader for Investopedia provides a detailed summary of day trading with over five-hour video-on-demand. During the course, you can learn everything from the order forms to the techniques of technical analysis to optimize your risk-adjusted returns.

Day Trading

As the name implies, it includes the establishment in a single day of hundreds of trade-based on technical research and sophisticated diagram systems. TTheday trader's goal is to survive off stocks, commodities, or currencies by small gains in various trades and the reduction of losses on unprofitable trade. Day traders do not typically hold positions or shares overnight.

The biggest benefit of day trading is the opportunity for incredible profits. But this could be only possible for a special person who has all the characteristics required, such as ambition, discipline, and dedication, to become a successful business owner.

The U.S. Securities-and-Exchange Commission (SEC) points out that "days traders usually lose money in their first months of trading and often never become profitable." While the SEC warns that day traders can only gamble money that they can afford to lose, many days traders experience significant losses on loans through disadvantaged trades and capital borrowed from family or other sources. Such losses will not only reduce their day-long business career but also put them in considerable debt.

The day trader operates alone, unaware of business bigwigs 'whims. It can take time off whenever it is needed and operate at its own speed, as opposed to anyone on the company's treadmill.

Day traders will deal with high-frequency traders, hedge funds, and other market professionals who invest millions on bust-of-the-art as no choice in this world but to invest heavily in a trading site, tools for tracking, state-of-the-art computers, and so on. The cost of receiving live quotes and commission expenses that may add up to the number of transactions are ongoing expenses.

Long-term traders like the excitement of the everyday challenge the market and other professionals. The rapid-fire trade adrenaline rush is something not many traders embrace, but it is a big deterrent in their decision to make a living from daytime trading. Doubtless, these people will be able to sell gadgets or poring numbers in an office cubicle for their days.

A day trader just wants to give up his day's work and give up his regular monthly paycheck. From then on, the day trader has to rely on his own ability and efforts to produce adequate income to pay the bills and to have a decent lifestyle.

Day trading is stressful as many screens need to look at opportunities for trading and move quickly to take advantage of them. This has to be done every day, and the need for such a high concentration and emphasis also contributes to burnout.

For many jobs in finance it is a requirement for interviews to have the appropriate degree from the right university. In comparison, day trading does not require expensive Ivy League school education. Although there are no specific qualifications for becoming a business day, technical analysis and computer trading courses can be very helpful.

- Day trading, as the name suggests, includes the creation, in one day, of hundreds of transactions, based on technical analysis and sophisticated charts.
- Swing trade is focused on the identification of stock, product, and currency variations over a period of days.
- No strategy should be better than the other, and traders should select the best solution to their talents, interests, and lifestyles.

Swing Trading

As rightly explained in the first chapter, this trading focused on the recognition of fluctuations in stocks, commodities, and currencies over many days. It could take a few days to a few weeks for a swing trade to work out. Unlike a day trader, a swing trade is unlikely to do a full-time job, although a trader may choose to be a day trader AND a swing trader.

Anyone with experience and capital investment will seek swinging trading. Because of the longer time span, a swing trader must not be connected all day long on his computer screen (from days to weeks to minutes to hours). He may also have a separate full-time job (unless he still searches on the trading screens at work).

Trade normally takes time to find out. Maintaining an asset exchange open for a couple of days or weeks could lead to more profitable trading in and out of the same protection many times a day.

Since swing trading typically requires at least overnight positions, there are higher margin requirements. Two times one's money is normally the optimum leverage. Compare this today trading where there are four times the capital margins.

The swing trader will estimate losses. Although there is a risk of stopping at an unfavorable price, it overcomes the constant monitoring of all open positions that are an important element of day trading.

Like any trading form, swing can also lead to major losses. Since swing traders are longer than day traders, they are in danger of losing more.

Since swing is rarely a full-time job, burnout is much less likely due to stress. Swing traders typically have a daily job or another revenue stream that compensates or mitigates trade losses.

Just one machine and traditional exchange tools can be used for swing trading. It does not need state-of-the-art day trading technology.

Main Differences

Trading day and swing trading each has advantages and inconveniences. Both approaches are no better than the other, so traders must agree on the strategy best suited to their skills, tastes such as lifestyles. The day trading system is more appropriate for people who are passionate about full-time trading and possess three Ds: decisiveness, discipline, and vigilance (prerequisites for day trading).

Success in day trading also needs a deeper understanding of technical trading and graphics. Due to the intense and stressful day trading, traders should be able to keep calm and control their emotions. Lastly, day trading involves risk — traders should sometimes be prepared to lose 100%.

Swing, however, does not require such an enormous set of features. As swing trading is possible for anybody with investment capital and needs no effort in full time, this is a viable option for traders who want to retain their full-time jobs but also have dabbled in the markets. Swing traders should also be willing, instead of technical analysis alone, to apply a mix of fundamental and technical analysis.

CONCLUSION

I hope this book has addressed some of your urgent questions about swing trading. Now let us complete it all by reiterating that you must settle for a style of trading that suits your personality. Swing trading increases day trading, as it helps you, the investor, to spend less time studying the markets every day. You do have a chance to gain money when you hold your company for more than a day.

Nonetheless, to be a good trader, you should be able to sacrifice a lot of time, wait longer for your business to be closed, and your emotions controlled. Overall, the rewards for swinging trading far outweigh the few inconveniences of this incredible style.

www.ingramcontent.com/pod-product-compliance
Lightning Source LLC
LaVergne TN
LVHW022059200926
848481LV00003B/983

* 9 7 9 8 2 0 1 3 8 4 9 8 2 *